Robert Ould, Confederate States of America Bureau of Exchange

Official Correspondence between the Agents of Exchange

Together with Mr. Ould's Report

Robert Ould, Confederate States of America Bureau of Exchange

Official Correspondence between the Agents of Exchange
Together with Mr. Ould's Report

ISBN/EAN: 9783337121525

Printed in Europe, USA, Canada, Australia, Japan

Cover: Foto ©ninafisch / pixelio.de

More available books at **www.hansebooks.com**

OFFICIAL CORRESPONDENCE

BETWEEN THE

AGENTS OF EXCHANGE,

TOGETHER WITH

MR. OULD'S REPORT.

RICHMOND:
SENTINEL JOB OFFICE.
1864.

REPORT

OF

COMMISSIONER OF EXCHANGE.

CONFEDERATE STATES OF AMERICA,
War Department,
Richmond, Va., Dec. 5th, 1863.

Hon. JAS. A. SEDDON, *Secretary of War:*

SIR: I have the honor to submit the accompanying correspondence between the Federal Agent of Exchange and myself:

I have selected from the mass of correspondence, such letters as relate to matters of general interest, and especially to the subjects of controversy between us.

1. Papers from one to twelve, inclusive, relate the arrest and detention of non-combatants. The Federal authorities have persistently refused to observe any reciprocal rule as to such parties. Their military commanders seem to have been permitted to make arrests of non-combatants without regard to their age, sex or situation. After arrest, they have been thrown into prison and there indefinitely retained, in most cases, without charges. I have persistently contended that the whole subject of their capture of non-combatants, should be determined by rule, and not by arbitrary practice. This reasonable proposal, not receiving the assent of the enemy, the Confederate authorities have been forced, in some instances, to retain Federal non-combatants as a measure of retaliation.

2. Papers from thirteen to sixteen, inclusive, relate to the retention of exchanged and unexchanged officers and men. There are officers and men now in Federal prisons, who have been there ever since the adoption of the cartel. I have brought to the attention of the United States authorities again and again the names of some of the parties who were confined in violation of the exchange agreements. In some cases, after long delay, the parties were released. Others, however, are still languishing in confinement.

3. Papers from seventeen to forty, inclusive, relate to the general orders of the enemy and their connection with declarations of exchange. So anxious has the Confederate Government been to remove all obstacles to a general exchange of prisoners, that when the

computation and adjustment of paroles was made a subject of difficulty by the enemy. we promptly agreed to determine the whole matter in accordance with the general orders, issued at Washington. This very liberal proposition has not been accepted by the Federal authorities. I have, however, by virtue of the provisions of the cartel, proceeded to make declarations of exchange, upon the basis of those general orders. In those declarations of exchange I have not exceeded the valid paroles, which are on file in my office. The reply of the Federal agent to my letter of October of last, 1863, was so personally offensive, that I was compelled to return it to him without my answer.

4. Papers from forty-one to forty-seven inclusive, relate to the confinement of Gen. John H. Morgan and his officers in the penitentiary, at Columbus, Ohio. Though the Federal agent on the 9th of July, 1863, notified me that Gen. John H. Morgan and his officers would be placed in close confinement, he did us two months afterwards, that "the United States authorities had nothing to do with the treatment that General Morgan and his command received when imprisoned at Columbus."

5. Papers from forty-eight to fifty-seven, inclusive, relate to the detention of surgeons. Before the date of the cartel, surgeons were unconditionally released after capture. That rule was first adopted by the Confederate commanders, and was subsequently followed by the Federals. Some time ago, one Rucker was indicted by a grand jury in Virginia, for several felonies. Although Rucker was never a surgeon in the Federal service, the enemy held surgeon Green, of the Confederate navy, in retaliation. This caused retaliation on our part, in return, and surgeons were afterwards held in captivity on both sides. In this instance, the Federal authorities proved that they were ready to sacrifice their own men in an endeavour to secure the release of a felon in no way connected with their medical service. Rucker having recently escaped from jail, the surgeons on both sides have been released.

6. Papers from fifty-eight to sixty-three, inclusive, relate to persons captured upon our rivers and the high seas. By agreement made with the Federal agent of exchange, all such who were captured before December 10th, 1862, were declared exchanged. In spite of that agreement, some of our pilots and sea captains were kept in confinement. The correspondence will fully show the refusal of the Federal authorities to adopt any fair and reciprocal rule, as to the further exchange of such persons.

7. Papers numbered sixty-four and sixty-five, show the pretensions of the enemy as to such persons as have been tried under the laws of a sovereign State for offences against the same.

8. Papers from sixty-six to seventy-two, inclusive, embrace all the correspondence in which Gen. E. A. Hitchcock has borne a part. It seems there are two commissioners of exchange, on the part of the Federal government. How far the authority of each extends, or how far one is subordinate to the other, has not as yet clearly appeared. The future may perhaps, explain that they may be put to separate

uses. The last letter of Gen. Hitchcock, bearing date November 23, 1863, I returned, with the following indorsement, to wit: "Protesting that the statement of facts contained in this paper is incorrect, I return it to its author as unfit to be either written or received."

With this brief notice of the correspondence, I respectfully submit it as my report.
Respectfullly,
Your obedient servant,
RO. OULD, *Agent of Exchange.*

CORRESPONDENCE

Relative to the Arrest and Detention of Non-Combatants.

[No. 1.]

MR. OULD TO LIEUT. COL. LUDLOW.

CONFEDERATE STATES OF AMERICA, WAR DEPARTMENT,
Richmond, Va., Oct. 4, 1862.

Lieut. Col. WM. H. LUDLOW,
Agent of Exchange:

SIR:

I also bring to your attention the case of peaceable, non-combatant citizens of the Confederate States, taken, in some instances, with almost every possible indignity, from their homes and thrown into military prisons. I do not utter it in the way of a threat, but candor demands that I should say, that if this course is persisted in, the Confederate Government will be compelled, by a sense of duty to its own citizens, to resort to retaliatory measures. In no one instance have the Confederate authorities sanctioned the arrest of any citizen of any one of the United States found in the exercise of a lawful and peaceful business. If such a case can be found, the wrong will be speedily righted. Such cases not being within the rules of military capture, are not, therefore, the proper subjects of exchange under a cartel. Hundreds of cases have been brought to the attention of the Confederate authorities, where parties in pursuit of their ordinary occupations, and not bearing arms, and not being in any military organization, have been arrested, dragged from their homes, and thrown into prisons, where they remain to this day, even though the United States forces, which made the arrest, have been withdrawn from the neighborhood where it was made. The Confederate Government can in no way, whether by a system of exchanges or otherwise, recognize the right of the United States to invade its territory, arrest, carry off, and detain indefinitely its peaceable citizens. In any case where an exchange is proposed, if the situation of the parties is the same, it will be cheerfully made. The Confederate Government, however, has not arrested your peaceable citizens, and has none of that class to offer in exchange for such of the Confederacy as have been taken. To exchange such as we have the right to capture, according to the usages of war, for our own peaceable citizens, unlawfully and unjustly taken, as we think, would be a *quasi* recognition of your right to make such captures. I trust, therefore, that the United States Government will unconditionally release all citizens of the Confederate States belonging to the class to which I have referred.

Very respectfully,
Your obedient servant,
RO. OULD, *Agent of Exchange.*

[No. 2.]

LIEUT. COL. LUDLOW TO MR. OULD.

HEADQUARTERS 7TH ARMY CORPS,
Fort Monroe, Va , Dec. 3, 1862.

Hon. ROBERT OULD,
Agent for Exchange of Prisoners:

SIR: Since I wrote to you this morning, information has been given me that some thirty or forty citizens of Pennsylvania, non-combatants, were seized by order of General Stewart, in his late incursion into Pennsylvania and Maryland, and were conveyed to Richmond. This is so clearly in contravention of the positions you have laid down, that I need only mention the fact to you to insure their immediate delivery to Capt. Mulford, in charge of the flag of truce.

I am, very respectfully,
Your obedient servant,
WM. H. LUDLOW,
Lieut. Col., and Agent for Exchange of Prisoners.

[No. 3.]

MR. OULD TO LIEUT. COL. LUDLOW.

RICHMOND, VA., Dec. 11, 1862.

Lieut. Col. WM. H. LUDLOW,
Agent of Exchange:

SIR: With reference to the Pennsylvania non-combatants captured by General Stewart, and whose release you ask in your letter of the 3d inst., I beg leave respectfully to state that they were captured, and are now held only in retaliation for captures of non-combatant citizens of the Confederate States. As soon as your Government releases the non-combatants of the Confederate States, now held by you, and agrees to abandon the policy of making such captures in the future, or, in other words, as soon as your Government agrees substantially to the proposition relating to such captures, which I made to you at our last interview, these citizens of Pennsylvania will be unconditionally released. You have in your military prisons at this time a far larger number of persons who were arrested on Confederate soil, while engaged in no acts of hostility to your Government, than we have in ours. How can you claim the release of your non-combatants when you retain ours? How can you ask us to release your non-combatants when you refuse to agree that ours shall not be captured? In retaining these Pennsylvanians, the Confederate Government does not abandon its position so often reiterated, that the capture of non-combatants is illegal, and contrary to the usages of civilized warfare. The Confederate Government is anxious to put an end to any such practice. It has protested earnestly and persistently against it. When those protests failed to accomplish the desired end, a sense of duty to its own citizens demanded that the Confederate Government should resort to other means. May I not hope that the United States Government will promptly settle this whole matter by a release of such Confederate citizens as are now in prison, and who, when captured, were connected with no military organization, and by a disavowal of any purpose to make any such arrests in the future?

Respectfully, your obedient servant,

RO. OULD, *Agent of Exchange.*

[No. 4.]

LIEUT. COL. LUDLOW TO MR. OULD.

HEADQUARTERS DEPARTMENT OF VIRGINIA, 7TH ARMY CORPS,
Fort Monroe, June 2, 1863.

Hon. ROBERT OULD,
Agent for Exchange of Prisoners:

SIR: A. D. Richardson and Junius H. Browne, correspondents of the New York *Tribune*, captured about the 4th of May last, near Vicksburg, are said to be confined in the Libby Prison. Mr. Colburn, the correspondent of the New York *World*, who was captured with them, has been released. It has been the practice to treat attaches of the press as non-combatants, and not to retain them. The release of Mr. Colburn is a partial recognition of this practice. Will you please inform me if you will release Richardson and Browne, and if not, why not.

I am, very respectfully,
Your obedient servant,
WM. H. LUDLOW,
Lieut. Col., and Agent for Exchange of Prisoners.

[No. 5.]
MR. OULD TO LIEUT. COL. LUDLOW.

Richmond, Va., *June* 5, 1863.

Lieut. Col. Wm. H. Ludlow,
  Agent of Exchange.

Sir: In one of your communications of the 2d, you refer to the correspondents of the press, and say it has been the practice "to treat them as non-combatants, and not to retain them." I have been struggling for nearly twelve months to establish just such a rule as to non-combatants, without success. The only difficulty I met, was in your consent. When was the rule established that non-combatants were not to be retained? What was the date of its adoption by Burnside, or Rosencrans, or Milroy? What peculiar immunity should the correspondents of the Tribune have over an old grey-headed grandfather, who never shouldered a musket, or followed in the wake of an army? Wherein are they privileged over delicate and noble-souled women, who are either languishing in your prisons or "released" to the rigors and dangers of the wilderness?

It seems to me that if any exception be made as to any non-combatants, it should be against such men as Tribune correspondents, who have had more share even than your soldiery in bringing rapine, pillage, and desolation to our homes. I have no compassion for any such, even if their miseries were ten-fold greater. You ask me why I will not release them. 'Tis because they are the worst and most obnoxious of all non-combatants. Yet, bad as they are, deeply as they have wronged and outraged us, they will be released if you will only discharge from imprisonment men and women "the latchets of whose shoes they are unworthy to unloose."

Mr. Colburn was released because Mr. Barr, a correspondent of the Grenada Appeal, was held by your authorities for one of the three correspondents, and it came within the rule of our "sovereign will and pleasure" to release him. Moreover, if I had been disposed to ignore Mr. Colburn, it would have given me a great deal of trouble to make a selection between the Tribune's correspondents.

Respectfully, your obedient servant,
  RO. OULD, *Agent of Exchange.*

[No. 6.]
MR. OULD TO BRIG. GEN. MEREDITH.

Richmond, Va., *August* 1, 1863.

Brig. Gen. S. A. Meredith,
  Agent of Exchange:

Sir:

* * * * * *

For the purpose of showing to you the position of the Confederate Government in relation to the imprisonment of non-combatants, I now renew to you the proposal which I have frequently tendered to your predecessor. I propose that all the non-combatants now held in prison, on either side, be immediately and unconditionally released; and that no captures of non-combatants shall hereafter be made. If the latter branch of this proposition is too broad, I will thank you to suggest any proper modification.

Respectfully, your obedient servant,

RO. OULD. *Agent of Exchange.*

[No. 7.]

BRIG. GEN. MEREDITH TO MR. OULD.

HEADQUARTERS DEPARTMENT OF VIRGINIA, 7TH ARMY CORPS,
Fort Monroe, August 27, 1863.

Hon. Robert Ould,
Agent of Exchange, Richmond, Va.:

SIR: I would again earnestly call your attention to the case of Messrs. Richardson and Brown, correspondents of the New York Tribune. In yours of August 20, you state "that there is no fair and reciprocal rule which may be proposed for mitigating the horrors of this war, that will not be cheerfully adopted by the Confederate authorities." Now, sir, I think that the Confederate authorities could not have a better opportunity for reciprocating, than in the case of the two gentlemen above named; for, when Vicksburg was captured, the editors of the Whig and Citizen fell into our hands, and were immediately paroled and sent away. If you are sincere, then, in your offers, I call upon you to give me evidence thereof, by immediately releasing Messrs. Richardson and Brown.

Respectfully, your obedient servant,

S. A. MEREDITH,
Brig. Gen., and Commissioner for Exchange.

[No. 8.]

MR. OULD TO BRIG. GEN. MEREDITH.

RICHMOND, *August* 28, 1863.

Brig Gen S. A. MEREDITH,
Agent of Exchange:

SIR: I still adhere to my declaration of the 20th instant, in respect to the release of non-combatants. To that, and almost every other communication involving a principle, you have not replied. Fairness requires that you should answer it, in some form, before you criticise it. Will you agree to the unconditional release of all non-combatants? Your reference to the parole of the editors of the Whig and Citizen, at Vicksburg, has no sort of force. They were paroled by the terms of surrender, and not by any special grace of your authorities. You could not have retained them without a breach of the terms of capitulation. Their cases are in no respect analagous to those of Richardson and Brown, except in their avocation of driving the quill. Richardson and Brown will be released just as soon as you agree to discharge non-combatants. I still say, there is no fair and reciprocal rule which may be proposed for mitigating the horrors of this war, that will not be cheerfully adopted by the Confederate authorities.

Respectfully, your obedient servant,

RO. OULD, *Agent of Exchange*

[No. 9.]

BRIG. GEN. MEREDITH TO MR. OULD.

HEADQUARTERS DEPARTMENT OF VIRGINIA, 7TH ARMY CORPS,
Fort Monroe, Aug. 14, 1863.

Hon. ROBERT OULD,
Commissioner for Exchange, Richmond, Va.:

SIR: Mr. Daniel Gerhart, an old and wealthy citizen of Ohio, was taken prisoner at Winchester, Va., while attending a son dangerously ill, and is now confined at Richmond. Can nothing be done to expedite the release of this gentleman?

Respectfully, your obedient servant,

S. A. MEREDITH,
Brig. Gen., and Commissioner for Exchange.

[No. 10.]

MR. OULD TO BRIG. GEN. MEREDITH.

RICHMOND, VA., *August* 20, 1863.

Brig. Gen. S. A. MEREDITH,
Agent of Exchange:

SIR: Your communication of the 14th instant, respecting Mr. Daniel Gerhart, has been received. You say he was taken prisoner at Winchester, while attending a son dangerously ill, and inquire whether anything can be done to expedite his release. Undoubtedly, something can be done. Release our non-combatants, whom you have in prison, and Mr. Gerhart is instantly free. I hope there is enough strength in Mr. Gerhart's case, he being a "wealthy citizen of Ohio," to accomplish what justice and mercy have asked in vain, for more than a year.

Respectfully, your obedient servant,
RO. OULD, *Agent of Exchange.*

[No. 11.]

BRIG. GEN. MEREDITH TO MR. OULD.

OFFICE COMMISSIONER FOR EXCHANGE,
Fortress Monroe, Va., Oct. 23, 1863.

Hon. ROBERT OULD,
Agent of Exchange, Richmond, Va.:

SIR: I enclose to you herewith, a letter from W. P. Wood, Superintendent of the Old Capitol Prison, addressed to Maj. Gen. E. A. Hitchcock, to which I specially call your attention.

Will you release our citizens, whom you hold confined in your prisons, against whom there are no charges? There is no disposition on the part of the United States authorities to harrass or annoy citizens. In all cases heretofore, so far as I know, whenever southern citizens have been arrested, it has been for special reasons, marking the individuals as seperated from the mass of a community. I know of no citizen of the South who is held by the United States authorities *merely* because he belongs to the South. If you know of any such, name them, and they shall be sent home. Some time since, the United States authorities arrested two citizens in Virginia, for special cause. The Richmond authorities arrested two supposed Union men, to answer for those mentioned above, without any charges against them. Why are not these men released? Within twenty-four hours after any given time, the United States authorities can arrest double or treble the number of citizens of the South, that you hold of citizens the North; and, though they have hitherto refrained from the arrest of citizens, as *such*, the detention of citizens in the Richmond prisons, or elsewhere in the South, as Union men, may necessitate a recourse to similar proceedings on the part of the authorities of the United States.

Should the infliction of such misery on the citizens of the South be inaugurated, on their own authorities will rest the onus.

Respectfully, your obedient servant,
S. A. MEREDITH,
Brig. Gen., and Commissioner for Exchange.

[No. 12.]

MR. OULD TO BRIG. GEN. MEREDITH.

CONFEDERATE STATES OF AMERICA, WAR DEPARTMENT,
Richmond, Va., Oct. 31, 1863.

Brig. Gen. S. A. MEREDITH,
Agent of Exchange:

SIR: In relation to your communication of the 23d instant, enclosing a letter from W. P. Wood to Gen. Hitchcock, I submit the following:

More than a year ago, recognizing the injustice of the arrest of non-combatants, I submitted the following proposition to the Federal authorities, to wit: "That peaceable, non-combatant citizens, of both the United States and the Confederate States, who are not connected with any military organization, shall not be arrested by either the United States or Confederate armies within the territory of the adverse party. If this proposition is too broad, let the only exception be the case of a temporary arrest of parties within army lines, where the arresting party has good reason to believe that their presence is dangerous to the safety of the army, from the opportunity afforded of giving intelligence to the enemy. It is to be understood, however, in the latter case, the arrest is to cease as soon as the reason for making it ceases, in the withdrawal of the army, or for any other cause. This proposal is understood to include such arrests and imprisonments as are already in force."

Although this proposition, so reasonable and humane in its terms, has been before your Government for more than a year, it has never been accepted. I now, again, invite your attention to it. If it does not suit you, I will thank you to suggest any modification. I am willing to adopt any fair and reciprocal rule that will settle this matter on principle. It must, however, be settled by rule. It cannot, with any safety, be determined by "special cases."

You ask me if I will release your citizens, against whom there are no charges. Would it not be more liberal to make that offer on your part, as far as our citizens are concerned, before you ask our consent? You have kept Confederate citizens in prison for many months, without charges. Most of them have never had any charges preferred against them, although, in the opinion of your authorities, there were "special reasons" for their arrest. How easy is it to give or invent a special reason? In all probability, there has never been an arrest and imprisonment, on either side, since this war began, for which there was not a "special cause." An arrest for retaliatory reasons, even, is special.

As far as the arrest of citizens of the Confederate States, by our authorities, is concerned, we will submit to no interference, in any way, by the Federal Government. It is a matter with which you have nothing to do. The Confederate authorities do not interfere with your arrests, of your own people, no matter what injustice has been done to them. Any attempt, on the part of the Federal Government, to interpose in cases which only concern our authorities, and the people of these Confederate States, may be justly styled impertinent and meddlesome. As far, however, as the arrests of citizens of the adverse party is concerned, we are, at all times, ready to adopt any fair and reciprocal rule.

Respectfully, your obedient servant,

RO. OULD, *Agent of Exchange.*

CORRESPONDENCE

Relative to the Retention of Exchanged and Unexchanged Officers and Men.

[No. 13.]

LIEUT. COL. LUDLOW TO MR. OULD.

HEADQUARTERS DEP'T OF VA., 7TH ARMY CORPS, }
Fort Monroe, Va., April 8, 1863. }

Hon. ROBERT OULD,
  Agent for Exchange of Prisoners:

SIR: The best mode of arranging all questions relating to exchange of officers, is to revoke, formally or informally, the offensive proclamation relating to our officers.

I simply ask that you say, by authority, that such proclamation is revoked. The spirit of that proclamation was the infliction of personal indignities upon our officers, and as long as it remains unrepealed, it can be at any moment put in force by your authorities. What assurance have we that it will not be?

I earnestly desire a return to the cartel in all matters pertaining to officers, and until such be the case, and uniformity of rule be thereby established, our exchanges of officers must be special. Some of our officers, paroled at Vicksburg, were subsequently placed in close confinement, and are now so held. If, hereafter, we parole any of your officers, such paroles will be offset against any which you may possess. At present the exchanges will be confined to such equivalents as are held in confinement on either side.

I hope you will soon be able to remove all difficulties about officers, by the revocation I have mentioned.

By reference to the map, you will see that Fort Delaware is en route to Fort Monroe. It is used as a depot for collecting of prisoners, sent from other places for shipment here, and is, from its peculiar position, "well adapted *for convenience for exchange.*"

If any mistake be found in the account of men paroled by Lieut. Col. Richards, at Oxford, Miss., on the 22d of December, 1862, it can be rectified when we meet.

I am, very respectfully, your obedient servant,
  WM. H. LUDDOW,
    Lieut. Col. and Agent for Exchange of Prisoners.

I have written to Mr. Hoffman to send T. J. Dunn, company F, 18th Mississippi regiment, and now said to be at Locust Springs.

[No. 14.]

MR. OULD TO LIEUT. COL. LUDLOW

Richmond, April 11th, 1863.

Lieut. Col. Wm. H. Ludlow,
    Agent of Exchange:

Sir: Your letters of the 8th instant have been received.

I am very much surprised at your refusal to deliver officers for those of your own who have been captured, paroled, and released by us, since the date of the proclamation and message of President Davis. That refusal is not only a flagrant breach of the cartel, but can be supported by no rule of reciprocity or equity. It is utterly useless to argue any such matter. I assure you that not one officer of any grade will be delivered to you, until you change your purpose in that respect.

You have charged us with breaking the cartel. With what sort of justice can that allegation be supported, when you delivered only a few days ago over ninety officers, most of whom had been forced to languish and suffer in prisons for months before we were compelled by that and other reasons to issue the retaliatory order of which you complain? Those ninety-odd are not one-half of those whom you unjustly hold in prison. On the other hand, I defy you to name the case of one who is confined by us, whom our agreement has declared exchanged. Is it your idea that we are to be bound by every strictness of the cartel, while you are at liberty to violate it for months, and that, too, not only in a few instances, but in hundreds? You know that our refusal to parole officers, was a matter exclusively of retaliation. It was based only upon your refusal to observe the requirements of the cartel. All that you had to do to remove the obnoxious measure of retaliation, was to observe the provisions of the cartel and redress the wrongs which had been perpetrated.

Your last resolution, if persisted in, settles the matter. You need not send any officers to City Point, with the expectation of getting an equivalent in officers, so long as you refuse to deliver any for those whom we have released on parole in Tennessee and Kentucky. If captivity, privation, and misery are to be the fate of officers on both sides hereafter, let God judge between us. I have struggled in this matter, as if it had been a matter of life and death to me. I am heartsick at the termination, but I have no self reproaches.

Respectfully, your obedient servant,
    ROBERT OULD,
        Agent of Exchange

[No 15.

MR. OULD TO BRIG. GEN. MEREDITH.

Richmond, Oct. 2d, 1863

Brigadier General S. A. Meredith,
Agent for Exchange:

Sir: I am very glad that Lieuts. Baker, Pumphrey, Crutcher, and Thorpe have at last been released. There are many other officers yet behind, precisely in their situation. I have frequently given a list of them to your predecessor. I will furnish you one if you desire it. You say the above-named have been detained by "some unaccountable mistake." Each of their names, with the places of confinement, has been more than once presented to the Federal agent. Lieut. Baker was at Fortress Monroe, the headquarters of the Agent of Exchange, for months. It is, indeed, "unaccountable."

I will make inquiry as to John W. Woolsey. Brengle did not belong to the sanitary commission. He was arrested upon his return from a difficult and hazardous military enterprise for which he was specially employed and paid. If you can bring him within the rule established as to members of the sanitary commission, I will release him.

Charles W. Webster is at Castle Thunder. He is a citizen, abiding in captivity until you release the non-combatants arrested on our soil and carried off to your prisons. I will make inquiry into the case of Henry D. Barnett.

Respectfully, your obedient servant,
ROBERT OULD,
Agent for Exchange.

[No. 16.]

MR. OULD TO BRIG. GEN. MEREDITH.

C. S. A., War Department,
Richmond, Va., Oct. 23, 1863.

Brig. Gen. S. A. Meredith,
Agent of Exchange:

Sir: Capt. Frank Battle, 20th regiment Tennessee volunteers, C. S. A., is now and has been for some time past in irons at Nashville. It is alleged that he is ironed in retaliation for similar treatment inflicted by the Confederate authorities, upon Capt. Shade Harris, company D, 3d East Tennessee cavalry, who was captured on or about the 26th of December, 1862. I have seen a special order, No. 51, issued by Brig. Gen. R. S. Granger, dated August 3d, 1863, in which it is directed that Capt. Battle shall be so treated and held.

Capt. Shade Harris, before he joined the Federal army, was a Confederate soldier. He deserted, and was subsequently captured in arms. For the crime of desertion, he was tried before a court martial, found guilty, and sentenced to death. Before conviction, he was neither closely confined or ironed. His father had access to him both before and after his trial. The President, in mercy, commuted the sentence to imprisonment. For that imprisonment your authorities have seen fit to put in irons and close imprisonment an officer captured in open warfare and against whom no personal charges have been preferred. I am very sure this statement is in entire conformity with the facts. If so, you deny our authority to try and punish a deserter from our army, even when the desertion is inflamed and made more heinous by direct support and succor to the enemy. I am strongly in hope that the mere statement of this case is sufficient to show the manifest wrong of the proceedings against Capt. Battle. I will thank you to inform me, if, upon the foregoing facts, your Government justifies its treatment of Capt. Battle, and whether you intend, by any form of retaliation upon our soldiers, to contest our right to punish desertion from our service, where the offending party has subsequently joined your army and been captured by our forces.

Respectfully, your obedient servant,

ROBERT OULD,
Agent of Exchange.

CORRESPONDENCE

Relative to the General Orders of the United States, and their connection with declarations of Exchange.

[No. 17.]

MR. OULD TO LIEUT. COL. LUDLOW.

RICHMOND, June 19, 1863.

Lieut. Col. WM. H. LUDLOW,
    Agent of Exchange:

SIR: On the 5th day of June, 1863, I requested you to inform me when general order, No. 100, was to be considered as going into effect. To that you have returned no answer. Its date is April 24, 1863. You delivered it to me on the 23d May, 1863.

I perceive by a general order, No. 15, March 9th, 1863, issued by General Schenck, that all officers and men, who had been captured in his department, and particularly in the Shenandoah Valley, and released on parole, and not regularly exchanged, should return to duty and service, on penalty of being considered deserters. When you delivered general order, No. 100, to me, I inquired of you as to the date when it went into effect. I understood you to say, the date of its delivery. You may, therefore, well imagine my surprise, when I perceive that by the general order of one of your departmental commanders, the new provisions as to paroles, are not only to have effect from and after March 9th, 1863, but are made to apply to all cases previous to that date, without any limitation as to time. This is not only contrary to your own declarations to me, but to our common practice up to May 23d, 1863. You have charged against me and received credit for several captures made by General Stoneman's command, in his recent raid. Is it pretended that you are to have credit for captures made by your commands, while none is to be given to us under precisely the same circumstances? Is this fair, or just, or right?

Respectfully, your obedient servant,
                                  RO. OULD,
                                 Agent of Exchange.

[No. 18.]

LIEUT. COL. LUDLOW TO MR. OULD.

HEADQUARTERS, DEPARTMENT OF VIRGINIA,
Seventh Army Corps,
Fort Monroe, July 7, 1863.

Hon. ROBERT OULD,
    Agent for Exchange of Prisoners :

SIR : I herewith enclose to you a copy of general order No. 207. which contains some additional provisions to those mentioned in my communication to you of the 22d May last. It is understood that officers of the United States, and Confederate officers have at various times and places paroled and released prisoners of war, not in accordance with the cartel.

The Government of the United States will not recognize, and will not expect the Confederate authorities to recognize, such unauthorized paroles. Prisoners released on parole, not authorized by the cartel. after my notice to you of the 22d May, will not be regarded as prisoners of war, and will not be exchanged.

When prisoners of war have been released without the delivery specified in the cartel, since the 22d May last, such release will be regarded as unconditional, and the prisoners released, as subject to orders without exchange, the same as if they had never been captured.

I am, very respectfully,
Your obedient servant,
WM. H. LUDLOW,
Lieut. Col. and Agent for Exchange of Prisoners.

[No. 19.]

WAR DEPARTMENT,
Adjutant General's Office,
Washington, D. C., July 3, 1863.

General Orders,
No. 207.

I. The attention of all persons in the military service of the United States, is called to article seven of the cartel, agreed upon on the 22d of July, 1862, and published in general orders No. 142, September 25th, 1862. According to the terms of this cartel, all captures must be reduced to actual possession, and all prisoners of war must be delivered at the places designated, there to be exchanged, or paroled until exchange can be effected. The only exception allowed is the case of commanders of two opposing armies, who are authorized to exchange prisoners, or to release them on parole at other points mutually agreed upon by said commanders.

II. It is understood that captured officers and men have been paroled and released in the field by others than commanders of opposing armies, and that the sick and wounded in hospitals have been so paroled and released, in order to avoid guarding and removing them, which, in many cases, would have been impossible. Such paroles are in violation of general orders and the stipulations of the cartel, and are null and void. They are not regarded by the enemy, and will not be respected in the armies of the United States. Any officer or soldier who gives such parole will be returned to duty without exchange, and, moreover, will be punished for disobedience of orders. It is the duty of the captor to guard his prisoners, and if, through necessity or choice he fail to do this, it is the duty of the prisoner to return to the service of his Government. He cannot avoid this duty by giving an unauthorized military parole.

III. A *military parole* not to serve till exchanged, must not be confounded with a *parole of honor* to do or not to do a particular thing not inconsistent with the duty of a soldier. Thus, a prisoner of war, actually held by the enemy, may, in order to obtain exemption from a close guard or confinement, pledge his parole of honor that he will make no attempt to escape. Such pledges are binding upon the individuals giving them, but they should seldom be given or received, for it is the duty of the prisoner to escape, if able to do so. Any pledge or parole of honor extorted from a prisoner by ill-usage or cruelty is not binding.

IV. The obligations imposed by the general laws and usages of war upon the non-combatant inhabitants of a section of country passed over by an invading army, cease when the military occupation ceases, and any pledge or parole given by such persons in regard to future service, is null and of no effect.

By order of the Secretary of War.

E. D. TOWNSSEND,
Assistant Adjutant General.

(Official copy,)
J. C. KELTON,
Assistant Adjutant General.

HEADQUARTERS ARMY, July 8, 1863.

[No. 20.]

MR. OULD TO LIEUT. COL. LUDLOW.

CONFEDERATE STATES OF AMERICA, WAR DEPARTMENT, }
Richmond, Va., July 13, 1863. }

Lieutenant Colonel WM. H. LUDLOW,
Agent of Exchange:

SIR: I have declared exchanged Lieutenant General Pemberton, Majors General Stevenson, Forney, M. L. Smith, and Bowen; Brigadier Generals Barton, Lee, Cumming, Moore, Hebert, Baldwin, Vaughan, and Shoup; Colonels Reynolds, Waul, and Cockerill; and Brigadier General Harris, of the Missouri militia; all of whom were recently captured and paroled at Vicksburg.

You can take the equivalents out of the officers captured and paroled by us at Chancellorsville, or from privates, as you prefer.

Respectfully,
Your obedient servant
RO. OULD,
Agent of Exchange.

[No. 21.]

LIEUT. COL. LUDLOW TO MR. OULD.

HEADQUARTERS DEP'T OF VIRGINIA, 7TH ARMY CORPS,
Fort Monroe, July 14, 1863.

Hon. ROBERT OULD,
Agent for Exchange of Prisoners:

SIR: I decline to unite with you in your declaration of the exchange of the officers named by you in your communication of the 13th instant, just received, and who form a part of those captured at Vicksburg.

In violation of the cartel, you now hold, in close confinement, many of our officers, though their release was long ago demanded, and their equivalents tendered to you. You even permitted these equivalents to be sent back to Fort Monroe from City Point. In this position of affairs, and being in entire ignorance of what you propose to do with our officers now in your hands, I must decline any special arrangements until we meet. This meeting, with your consent, will take place as soon as I shall have received the paroles of the Vicksburg captures.

Please, therefore, notify the officers named by you, that their exchange cannot be recognized by our authorities, until the declarations be united in by me.

In making arrangements with you for exchanges of paroles of officers, I shall expect to exhaust equivalents of equal rank, before we take up those of higher rank.

To settle all difficulties connected with exchanges of officers, I again invite you to a return to the cartel, and if you refuse, I again ask you, why such refusal.

I am, very respectfully,
Your obedient servant,
WM. H. LUDLOW,
Lieutenant Colonel, and Agent for Exchange of Prisoners.

The declaration of exchange made by you on the 2d instant, leave you in debt to me between eight and nine hundred men. Please make no more declarations until we meet.

[No. 22.]

MR. OULD TO LIEUT. COL. LUDLOW.

RICHMOND, July 17, 1863.

Lieutenant Colonel WM. H. LUDLOW,
Agent of Exchange:

SIR: In my communication to you of the 13th instant, declaring the exchange of certain officers who had been captured and paroled at Vicksburg, I only did what you yourself have frequently done. On at least one occasion, you went farther than I presumed to go You declared your men exchanged, when you had no equivalents to offer. You say in your letter of the 14th instant, that you decline to unite with me in my declaration, and request me to notify the officers that their exchange cannot be recognized. I call your attention to the fifth article of the cartel, which provides that "each party upon the discharge of prisoners of the other party, is authorized to discharge an equal number of their own officers or men from parole." I have exercised a clear right under the cartel—one that you have exercised over and over again. I have already delivered to you the equivalents of these officers, which equivalents you may declare exchanged. My right to declare these officers exchanged does not depend upon your assent. After I have given you equivalents, their exchange is perfected by my declaration, whether you "decline to unite" with me or not. I shall not, therefore, give the notice which you request. The officers referred to are already rightfully and properly exchanged. The right to declare officers and men exchanged where equivalents have been delivered, is one that I cannot yield, and I am unwilling to bind myself by an agreement not to exercise that right "until we meet."

Respectfully, your obedient servant,

RO. OULD,
Agent of Exchange.

[No. 23.]

LIEUT. COL. LUDLOW TO MR. OULD.

New York, July 22, 1863.

Hon. Robert Ould,

Agent for Exchange of Prisoners:

Sir: Your communication of the 17th instant has been forwarded to me here.

There is no authority in the cartel for your proposed declaration of exchange of your officers captured at Vicksburg, in the manner you indicate. The cartel provides for exchanges of equal rank, until such are exhausted, and then for equivalents.

In consequence of the very much larger number of officers and men we hold on parole and in confinement, you can give no equivalents for the general officers you desire to have exchanged. You cannot, for a moment, assume that you can select a general officer, and declare his equivalents in those of inferior rank, when we hold the paroles of your officers of the same rank as the latter. But even supposing this arrangement was permitted by the cartel, I do not see how you could avail yourself of it at this time. You will recollect that since the proclamation of the Hon. Jefferson Davis, of December last, and more especially since the passage of the act of your Congress in reference to our captured officers, both of which were in violation of the cartel, and have caused in the one case a temporary, and in the other a continued suspension of exchanges of officers under the cartel that all such exchanges have been subjects of special agreement between us. To avoid the complication and annoyance of these special agreements, I have again and again urged you to a return to the cartel, but up to the present moment in vain. On the contrary, you retain in close confinement large numbers of our officers for whom I have made a demand and tendered equivalents. Until you consent to a return to the terms prescribed by the cartel for exchanges of officers, I shall not consent to any exchanges of them, except on special agreements.

I repeat that I decline to unite in your proposed declaration of exchange of officers captured at Vicksburg, and if recaptured they will be dealt with as violators of their parole.

Ought you not, in justice to them, to notify them of the exact condition of their cases, and thus enable them to avoid being placed in a false position.

If you are authorized to deliver our officers now held in close confinement, and to a return to the cartel in exchanges of all officers, all the complicated questions which have arisen within the last few months can be promptly disposed of. To such a return, in the name of humanity, I again invite you. I am now only waiting the receipt of papers, connected with the Vicksburg captures, before going to City Point.

    I am, very respectfully,
        Your obedient servant,
            WM. H. LUDLOW,
    Lieutenant Colonel, and Agent of Exchange of Prisoners.

[No. 24.]

MR. OULD TO LIEUT. COL. LUDLOW.

CONFEDERATE STATES OF AMERICA, WAR DEPARTMET,
        Richmond, Va., July 26th, 1863.

COL. WM. H. LUDLOW,
    Agent of Exchange:

SIR: Your communication of the 22nd contests my declaration of exchanges of officers made on the 17th instant. You say "the cartel provides for the exchange of equal ranks, until such are exhausted, and then for equivalents." If you had been at Fortress Monroe, where you could have seen the cartel, instead of New York, from which your letter is dated, you would have written no such paragraph. There is nothing in the cartel which contains any such doctrine, or which favors it. Every provision is against it. Your own and my practice have been opposed to it. I again say to you what I have already stated in my communication of the 17th instant, that your assent is not needed to the declared exchange, and I shall not notify the officers, whom I have declared exchanged, as you request. I have allowed you to declare exchanges when the number of prisoners in our hands has been the greater. This has been the case from the day when we first met in the fall of last year, to the capture at Vicksburg. Now, when you have scarcely received official advices of your superiority in prisoners, you boast of the fact, and declare that I cannot give an equivalent for the general officers I have declared exchanged. The point you make is worth nothing, even as you have stated it. You know we have no Lieutenant Generals or Major Generals of yours in our hands. For that reason I have declared them exchanged in privates or inferior officers at your election. I had the right, under the cartel, to make the choice myself, but I preferred that you should do it, and, therefore, I gave you the notification which I did. If, at any time, you present officers for exchange who have been paroled, and we have no officers of similar rank on parole, you can declare their exchange in privates. If, it at this time, you have any officers of the rank I have declared exchanged, or of any other rank, or if you have any particular organization of privates or non-commissioned officers whom you wish exchanged, you have only to state such fact and your selection will be approved. If you hold the paroles of our officers of any rank as you state, you have only to present them, and whatever is in our hands, whether on parole or in captivity, will be freely given in exchange for them. You say you have again and again invited me to a return to the cartel. Now that our official connection is being terminated, I say to you in the fear of God—and I appeal to Him for the truth of the declaration—that there has been no single moment, from the time when we were first brought together in connectoin with the matter of exchange to the present hour, during which there has not been an open and notorious violation of the cartel, by your authorities Officers and men, numbering over hundreds, have been, during your whole connection with the cartel, kept in cruel confinement, sometimes in irons, or doomed to cells, without charges or trial. They are in prison now, unless God, in His mercy, has released them. In our parting moments, let me do you the justice to say that I do not believe it is so much your fault as that of your authorities. Nay more, I believe your removal from your position has been owing to the personal efforts you have made for a faithful observance, not only of the cartel, but of humanity in the conduct of the war.

Again and again have I importuned you to tell me if one officer or man now held in confinement by us, who was declared exchanged. You have, to those appeals, furnished one, Spencer Kellog. For him I have searched in vain. On the other hand, I appeal to your own records for the cases where your reports have shown that our officers and men have been held for long months and even years in violation of the cartel and our agreements. The last phase of the enormity, however, exceeds all others. Although you have many thousands of our soldiers now in confinement in your prisoners, and especially in that horrible hold of death, Fort Deleware, you have not, for several weeks, sent us any prisoners. During those weeks you have dispatched Captain Mulford with the steamer New York to City Point, three or four times without any prisoners. For the first two or three times some sort of an excuse was attempted. None is given at this present arrival. I do not mean to be offensive when I say that effrontery could not give one. I ask you with no purpose of disrespect, what can you think of this covert attempt to secure the delivery of all your prisoners in our hands, without the release of those of ours who are languishing in hopeless misery in your prisons and dungeons?

    Respectfully,
        Your obd't serv't,
         ROB'T. OULD,
         Agent of Exchange.

[No. 25.]

EXCHANGE NOTICE, No. 6.

RICHMOND, September 12, 1863.

The following confederate officers and men, captured at Vicksburg. Miss., July 4, 1863, and subsequently paroled have been duly exchanged, and are hereby so declared:

1. The officers and men of Gen. C. L. Stevenson's division.
2. The officers and men of Gen. Bowen's division.
3. The officers and men of Brig. Gen. Moore's brigade.
4. The officers and men of the 2d Texas regiment.
5. The officers and men of Waul's legion.
6. Also, all confederate officers and men who have been delivered at City Point at any time previous to July 25th, 1863, have been duly exchanged, and are hereby so declared.

RO. OULD, *Agent of Exchange.*

[No. 26.]

BRIG. GEN. MEREDITH TO MR. OULD.

HD. QRS. DEPT. OF VA., SEVENTH ARMY CORPS.
Fortress Monroe, September 24th, 1863.

Hon. ROBT. OULD, *Agent, &c:*

SIR: To meet your declaration of exchange of the 12th instant, I inform you that I have this day announced the following:

"A declaration of exchange having been announced by R. Ould, Esq., agent for exchange at Richmond, Va., dated September 12, 1863, to meet the same in part, as equivalents, it is hereby declared that all officers and men of the United States army captured and paroled at any time previous to the 1st September, 1863, are duly exchanged.

S. A. MEREDITH,
Brigadier General, Commissioner for Exchange."

The number of officers covered by the first five sections of your declaration is	1,208	
The number of enlisted men is		14,865
The number of officers covered by 6th section is	72	
The number of enlisted men is		8,014
Making a total of officers,	1,280	
And total of enlisted men,		22,879

Aggregate.	24,159	
Reduced to enlisted men,		29,133
Of the Federal troops on parole there are		
Officers.	76	
Enlisted men,	19,083	
Aggregate,	19,159	
Reduced to enlisted men,		19,409
Which gives a balance in our favor, of		10,024

I now claim this balance which is due us, and I demand that you return to their paroles all officers and men for whom you have paroled no equivalents, or that you release an equal number from the prisons in Richmond.

Your declaration was wholly unwarranted under the cartel, and it might with great propriety be set aside. In it you failed to announce to me the 6th section, as published in the Richmond Enquirer of the 10th instant, which covers 72 officers and 8,014 enlisted men. You did not, according to the terms of the cartel, furnish me with any "list," or even give me the number of men, by which I could declare equivalents, nor did you give me any time to prepare my announcement. I here deem it incumbent upon me to state that I consider your course in this matter a deliberate breach of good faith on the part of the authorities under whom you act. The 5th article of the cartel (General Orders, No. 142, 1862,) would have authorized you to discharge prisoners of the Federal forces, furnishing a "list" of them, and then you could have discharged an equal number of your own officers and men "from parole." The cartel not only contemplates a "mutual" exchange of "lists" (article 5), but expressly declares (article 4) that no exchange is to be considered complete until the officer or soldier exchanged for has been actually restored to the lines to which he belongs.

As to the paroles given at Gettysburg and elsewhere, you made an agreement with my predecessor, Lieut. Col. Ludlow, to take effect from May 22d, 1863, that all paroles given not in accordance with the cartel, should be considered null and void. How, then, can you claim as valid the Gettysburg paroles?

If you have any rolls or lists of any men whom you have paroled that I have not given you credit for, or if there should be any errors in my account, I will be happy to rectify the same.

You declared exchanged, before my predecessor was relieved, certain officers captured at Vicksburg, in which declaration he refused to unite. There are but two officers, I believe (Generals Stevenson and Bowen), who are covered by your declaration of the 12th instant. If the other officers named have not been returned to their paroles, as requested by Lieut. Col. Ludlow, you are indebted to us for their equivalents. The chief ground of the objection to that declaration, that at that time there were no equivalents of the same grade in our possession (the only condition which would have warranted your making the declaration); and if we consented to it we would be obliged to offset them by officers of inferior rank.

In making up the number of Federal troops to be exchanged, I have included all those mustered out of the service, all discharged, deserted and deceased.

Respectfully, your obedient servant,
S. A. MEREDITH,
Brigadier General and Commissioner of Exchange.

[No. 27.]

MR. OULD TO BRIG. GEN. MEREDITH.

RICHMOND, *Oct.* 2, 1863.

Brig. Gen. S. A. MEREDITH,
    Agent of Exchange:

SIR: Your communication of the 24th ultimo, declaring that all officers and men of the United States army, captured and paroled at any time previous to the 1st of September, 1863, are duly exchanged, has been received.

You are aware that when I met you on the 24th of August last, at City Point, I made to you the following proposal, to wit: "I propose that all paroles, on both sides, heretofore given, shall be determined by the General Orders issued by the War Department of the United States, to wit: No. 49, No. 100, and No. 207, of this year, according to their respective dates, and in conformity with paragraph 131 of General Order No. 100, so long as said paragraph was in force. If this proposition is not acceptable, I propose that the practice heretofore adopted respecting paroles and exchanges, be continued. In other words, I propose that the whole question of paroles be determined by the General Orders of the United States, according to dates, or that it be decided by former practice." You have neither accepted or declined either branch of that proposal, although I have, both in personal interview and by letter, solicited you to do one or the other. On the same day you submitted to me your proposition, which, unlike mine, was prepared before hand, and which is as follows: "I propose, on behalf of the Government of the United States, that all paroles given by officers and men between the 23d day of May, 1863, and the 3d day of July, 1863, not in conformity with the stipulations of the cartel, shall be regarded as null and void. A declaration to this effect to be published to both armies." That proposition I immediately declined. I then and there gave you my reasons. In the first place, I informed you that the Confederate authorities had never, at any time, and did not then ask that paroles, "not in conformity with the stipulations of the cartel," should be regarded as valid. I further told you that an agreement to regard "as null and void" paroles between certain dates, which were "not in conformity with the stipulations of the cartel," was an implication that paroles liable to the same objection before the first named date and after the last, *should* be regarded as valid, and was, therefore, necessarily vicious on its very face. I also told you that another reason for declining your proposition, was the one which caused you to make it, to wit: that the paroles which had been given to us were *between* the dates embraced in your proposition, while those given to you were before and after. When I made the objection to your proposal, that it intimated that paroles "not in conformity with the stipulations of the cartel" before the 23d of May, and after the 3d of July, of this year, were to be regarded as valid, I asked you to state, in writing, that no such intimation was conveyed. This you declined to do, saying, somewhat brusquely, that you did not wish to have any discussion about the matter. Upon my pressing the subject, however, you put a memorandum at the foot of the proposition, saying that the proposal was in reply to my letter of August 5, 1863, and in lieu of the proposition therein made by me. You would not, did not disclaim the implication which your proposition contained, nor have you done so since. My letter of the 5th of August only demanded, in compliance with your own General Order, No. 100, that if you rejected the paroles, the parties should be delivered to us.

You informed me that you would transmit my proposition to Washington, and give me a speedy answer in person or by letter.

On the 7th of September I complained that no reply had been returned, although two weeks had elapsed, and two boats had been dispatched to City Point since the date of our interview. At the same time I informed you that the Confederate authorities would consider themselves entirely at liberty to pursue any course with reference to my proposition which they might deem right and proper under all the circumstances of the case.

Accordingly, on the 11th of September, in pursuance of this plain intimation, I notified you that on the following day (that being the time when the notice would reach you) I would declare exchanged a portion of the Vicksburg captures. I gave you the divisions, brigades, regiments and batteries. I also informed you that I had in my possession more valid paroles of your officers and men than would be an equivalent for the exchange I then declared; that, in addition, I had delivered at City Point some ten or twelve thousand men since the last declaration of exchange; that, as it had been the practice, however, of the agents of exchange, whenever one of them declared a special exchange, to allow the other to select the equivalents, I gave you that privilege, and if you did not avail yourself of it, I would name the Federal officers and men who were discharged from their parole by reason of the declaration of exchange then made. This notification to you was not only in accordance with former practice, but was sanctioned if not demanded by the fifth article of the cartel, which, after providing for the manner in which "each party" may discharge "their" officers and men from parole, says, "thus enabling *each* party to relieve from parole such of *their own* officers and men as the party may choose." I have said this course was in accordance with former practice, and for proof, refer you to the letters of Lieut. Col. Ludlow, former agent of exchange, of the following dates of this year, to wit: April 6th, 8th, 13th, 19th and 27th; May 12th, 26th and 30th; June 5th, 9th and 13th, wherein he declared the exchange of Federal officers and men.

In one of Lieut. Col. Ludlow's communications of May 30, 1863, he says: "I have declared exchanged the Holly Springs capture, the 91st regiment Illinois volunteers, captured at Elizabethtown, Ky., December 27, 1862, and the captures at Mt. Sterling, on the 22d and 23d of March, 1863; also, the officers and men of the Indianola. The exact numbers I have not on hand, but they foot up some hundreds less than the balance due. I will furnish you with the exact numbers as soon as received." The same boat that conveyed that communication brought another written subsequently, but dated the same day, as follows: "I have declared exchanged the 51st regiment Indiana volunteers, 73d regiment Indiana volunteers, and 3d regiment Ohio volunteers. These number each less than three hundred men, and compose a part of Streight's brigade. I will add to the above declaration the 80th Illinois volunteers, and fifty-eight members of the 1st Tennessee cavalry."

The enlisted men alone, designated in *either one* of the communications, exceeded the "balance" due to Lieut. Col. Ludlow. The excess in both communication was two thousand two hundred and ninety, without taking into account "the captures at Mt. Sterling on the 22d and 23d of March, 1863."

You will observe that Lieut. Col. Ludlow, in these two communications, "did not furnish me with any list, or even give me the number of men, by which I could declare equivalents; nor did he give me any time to prepare my announcement." I quote from your letter of the 24th of September to me.

Not only was that the case, but he made a wholesale exchange of the Mt. Sterling captures, by a simple reference to it as being made "on the 22d and 23d day of March, 1863," without any designation of corps, division, brigade, regiment or company. Further than that, I have never, to this day, been furnished with a list of those captured at Mt. Sterling, or even with the aggregate number.

Such, then, were the circumstances, and such the precedents, under which I declared the exchanges of September 12, 1863. I have purposely gone into minute and faithful detail in consequence of the extraordinary character of your letter of the 24th of September. You state that you consider my course to be a deliberate breach of good faith on the part of the authorities under whom I act. In a bungling sort of way you have used language which casts an offensive aspersion both upon myself and the Government I represent. If there had not been subjects of very grave import to both people referred to in other portions of your communication, I would have treated it with the silent contempt it deserved, and returned it to you without comment. For the first time in the correspondence of the agents of exchange has any such discourtesy occurred. I regret it very much. Heretofore I have had occasion to complain of the action of your Government, but it has always been done with decorum. I have never written a word personally offensive to the Federal agent of exchange, or insulted his Government with a charge of "*deliberate* breach of good faith." It is a matter of very little moment to me what may be your opinion of "my course." There are some people connected with this war who, either from ignorance or passion, seem to have no clear ideas on any subject. The opinion of such, even if uttered in the language of courtesy, is but of little avail, but, if expressed with intemperance, only "exalts their folly." There has been no breach of faith on the part of the Confederate States, "deliberate" or otherwise. You were importuned to agree to some fair principle by which paroles could be adjusted and computed. After patient waiting—after failure on your part to respond affirmatively or negatively—the Confederate Government, through its agent of exchange, did what was demanded by courtesy, and justified both by former practice and the provisions of the cartel.

I now proceed to notice the misstatements of your letter. I will not call them "deliberate," although you had the means of correcting them at your hand; for such phraseology, so open to the imputation of discourtesy and coarseness, finds in such communications as the present only the precedent of your example.

1. Your computation of paroles is incorrect on both sides. As to your item of 1,208 officers and 14,865 men, embraced by the first five sections of my exchange notice, I have no exception to make. Some of our Vicksburg rolls were lost, and I have not the means of making an accurate computation as to them.

Your second item, however, of 72 officers and 8,014 men, embracing the sixth section of my exchange notice, is incorrect. In the first place, all the officers *on both sides*, who have been delivered at City Point, are exchanged. They were specially exchanged. Major Mulford knows that fact. All Confederate soldiers who were delivered at City Point up to May 23, 1863, including said date, were declared exchanged by Lieut. Col. Ludlow, while the Federal troops were only exchanged up to May 6, 1863. The number of Confederate soldiers, reduced to privates, delivered at City Point from May 23 to July 25, (the date named in my notice,) is 5,831, instead of 8,014. The rolls show this very clearly. Of the Federal troops on parole, you say there are 76 officers and 19,083 men. If these officers are those delivered at City Point, you make an error against yourself. They have been exchanged. From the 6th of May, 1863, (the time of the last exchange of Federal troops,) to the 1st of September, 1863, (the time named in your notice,) I have delivered at City Point alone, in privates, 18,610. All of these are on parole. I have other valid paroles in my possession, amounting to at least 16,000 more. Allowing, therefore, that your Vicksburg computation is correct, you owe me, upon the last notice which you have published, more than 7,000, instead of my owing you 10,024, as you claim. Many of the 16,000 paroles to which I have referred, have been acknowledged by Lieut.

Col. Ludlow in his correspondence. So much as to your computation, and your exchange notice based upon it.

2. You say I failed to announce to you "the sixth section of my exchange notice, as published in the Richmond Enquirer of the 10th instant, which covers 72 officers and 8,014 enlisted men." This is not so. On the 1st of August last I informed you in writing that I had declared exchanged all Confederate soldiers who had been delivered at City Point up to July 20, 1863. No deliveries were made at City Point between July 20 and July 25, and therefore one announcement was the same as the other. I did not inform you of the exchange of the City Point men in my letter of the 11th September, because I had already notified you on the 1st of August.

3. You say I did not furnish you with any list, or even give the number of men, by which you could declare equivalents, nor did I give you any time to prepare your announcement. You were furnished with the lists of all paroled men delivered at City Point, numbering up to September 1, 18,610 men. As to other paroles held by me, you failed to accept or decline the terms upon which they were to be computed and adjusted, and therefore it was useless to send them. You had, or ought to have had, duplicates of many of them in your possession. If there was any particular capture on parole, or any special class of paroled men whom you wished to declare exchanged, you had only to announce that fact, and the lists would be furnished if I had them and you had not. With what propriety could I send you lists which I believed to be in accordance with the cartel, but which you intimated you would decline to acknowledge? Moreover, according to my interpretation of the cartel, that instrument very clearly gives the right to you to select what Federal officers and men shall be relieved from their parole, whenever I discharge our officers and men from their parole. I claim the same right when you declare an exchange of your paroled men. If I had sent you lists of such of your officers and men as were relieved from their parole by my declaration of exchange, I would, in effect, have violated that provision of the cartel which gives the right to "each party to relieve from parole such of their own officers and men as the party may choose." It was entirely unnecessary for me to give you the number of men whom my notice declared exchanged. They were all Vicksburg captures or City Point deliveries. You had the rolls of both. You had in your possession as much information as I could communicate, even if I had held the Vicksburg rolls, which I did not. I have already proved to you by the record that the former Federal agent, when he declared exchanges, gave neither lists nor the number of men. There is, however, a more recent case. You yourself have just declared a sweeping exchange. You have not furnished me with any lists or designation of corps, division, brigade, regiment, or company, notwithstanding the clamor you have raised about my omission in those particulars. Your objection as to want of time for the preparation of your announcement, is a small one at best. The cartel does not make it incumbent upon me to give you time. Your predecessor did not give it to me. The correspondence, however, between us, before the 12th

of September, was of such a nature as must have prevented a surprise.

4. I did not make any such agreement with your predecessor, Lieut. Col. Ludlow, as you state, nor did I ever make any agreement with any one, by which I renounced the right to claim the paroles given at Gettysburg. The first official letter which I ever addressed to you was in relation to this very subject. It bears date August 1, 1863, and is as follows:

"BRIG. GEN. S. A. MEREDITH,
"*Agent of Exchange:*

"SIR: In the Army and Navy Official Gazette of the date of July 14th, 1863, I find a letter from Lieut. Col. Wm. H. Ludlow, of the date of July 7th, 1863, addressed to Col. J. C. Kelton. In it is the following paragraph, to wit:

"'I have the honor also to state that since the 22d of May last, it has been distinctly understood between Mr. Ould and myself, that all captures must be reduced to possession, and that all paroles are to be disregarded unless taken under the special arrangement of commanding officers of armies in the field, as prescribed in section seven of the cartel.'

"If Lieut Col. Ludlow means that he had declared to me that such was the rule which had been adopted by the United States in relation to captures and paroles, to go into effect from and after May 23d, 1863, he is entirely right. If he means that I at any time consented to adopt or acquiesce in any such rule, he is entirely wrong. All that passed between us on that subject is in writing. The correspondence will interpret itself.

"Respectfully, your ob't. serv't.,
"ROB'T. OULD,
"*Agent of Exchange.*"

The general order, No. 100, issued at Washington, which Lieut. Col. Ludlow communicated to me on the 23d May, 1863, in its 131st paragraph provides, that "if the Government does not approve of the parole, the paroled officer must return into captivity; and should the enemy refuse to receive him, he is free of his parole." In no communication, in no interview with either Lieut. Col. Ludlow or yourself, where the subject was under consideration, did I ever fail to demand that, if your Government rejected the paroles, the parties should return into captivity. I had the warrant of your own general order for that demand, but pleaded it in vain. So far from carrying out its own general order, your Government, on the 30th June last, while the order was in force, and before the publication of general order, No. 207, convened a court of enquiry, and required the court to give its opinion on the following point, to wit: whether Major Duane and Captain Michler, captured and paroled on the 28th June, 1863, should be placed on duty without exchange, or be required to return to the enemy as prisoners of war. The general order required the latter; but the court found that the Government was free to place those officers on duty without exchange. The reason given by the court was, not that the Federal agent and myself had *agreed* to regard such paroles as invalid, but that I had been *notified* they would not be recognized. It is true that I was informed that certain paroles would not be considered as valid, but I was also notified at the same time, by the same hand, and through the same instrument, that the "paroled officer" must return into captivity if his parole was not approved. In other words, on that day (May 23d, 1863,) Lieut. Col. Ludlow, with little or no comment, delivered to me general order, No. 100, as the rules adopted for the government of the Federal army. I never had any intimation that all the provisions of general order, No. 100, did not continue in force, until I received, on the 8th of July, 1863, the following letter from Lieut. Col. Ludlow:

"FORT MONROE, July 7th, 1863.

"SIR: I herewith enclose to you a copy of general order, No. 207, which contains some additional provisions to those mentioned in my communication to you of the 22d May last. It is understood that officers of the United States and Confederate officers have, at various times and places, paroled and released prisoners of war, not in accordance with the cartel.

"The Government of the United States will not recognize, and will not expect the Confederate uthorities to recognize such unauthorized paroles. Prisoners released on parole not authorized by the cartel, after my notice to you of the 22d May, will not be regarded as prisoners of war, and will not be exchanged.

"Where prisoners of war have been released without the delivery specified in the cartel, since the 22d of May last, such release will be regarded as unconditional, and the prisoners released as subject to orders without exchange, the same as if they had never been captured.

"I am, very respectfully,
"Your obedient servant,
"WM. H. LUDLOW.
"*Lieut. Col. and Agent for Exchange of Prisoners.*

"Hon. ROB'T. OULD, *Agent, &c.*"

The "notice" referred to in Lieut. Col. Ludlow's letter was the delivery of general order, No. 100, with its 131st paragraph. That paragraph was set aside by the provisions of general order, No. 207, which bears date July 3, 1863, three days *after* the submission of the question of the paroles of Duane and Michler to the court of inquiry, two days *after* its finding, and several days *after* our captures in the Gettysburg campaign. On the 7th of July, 1863, Lieut. Col. Ludlow substantially informs me that although he notified me on the 22d of May, that paragraph 131 of general order, No. 100, was to be continued in force; yet, under the circumstances of the case, and in view of what had taken place in Maryland and Pennsylvania, said paragraph was not to be considered as being in force at any time after the 22d of May, and general order, No. 207, although it was issued July 3, 1863, should be construed as bearing date the 22d of May, preceding!

It will be observed that Lieut. Col. Ludlow, in his letter to me of the 7th of July, no where says I had made any agreement with him, and yet it bears the same date as his letter to Col. Kelton. It is apparent on the face of the paper that he is conveying to me certain information for the first time, and that this information is the "additional provisions" of general order, No. 207, one of which set aside paragraph 131 of general order, No. 100. The court of enquiry, in its finding, (see Army and Navy Official Gazette, July 14, 1863,) says I was "*notified*," &c. Lieut. Col. Ludlow, in his letter to Col. Kelton, says it was distinctly "*understood*" between Mr Ould and himself, &c. You, in your letter of the 24th of September, say I made an "*agreement*" with your predecessor. The notification first rises to an understanding, and is then elevated into an agreement. What further promotion it will receive remains to be seen.

You have charged a deliberate breach of good faith upon the part of the Confederate States. Let me bring to your attention an incident connected with this matter of release from paroles. On March 9, 1863, General Schenck, of immortal memory, issued a general order, No. 15, requiring all officers and men who had been captured and paroled in his department, and particularly in the Shenandoah Valley, but who had not been exchanged, to return to duty on penalty of being considered deserters. Your general order in force at that time—No. 49, February 28, 1863—in section 8, provided that if the engagement which a prisoner made was not approved by his Government, he was bound to return and surrender himself as a prisoner of war. The same general order, No. 49, in the same section 8, uses these memorable words, which I now set up against your present extraordinary claims, to wit: "His own Government cannot, at the same time, disown his engagement and refuse his return as a prisoner." In spite of those honest words, General Schenck issued his order, which to this day has not been countermanded, in effect directing not only that such as were captured and paroled after March 9th, 1863, should return to duty, but also all who had been captured and paroled, under the circumstances named, since the beginning of hosilities, on penalty of being considered deserters. At that very time and afterwards, even to as late as Stoneman's raid, the former agent of exchange was charging against me, and receiving credit for captures and paroles similar to those repudiated by Schenck's order. It is due to Lieut. Col. Ludlow that I should say that, when the matter was brought to his attention, he declared that Schenck's action was without proper authority, and that I would have credit for such as reported for duty under the order. Still the order was not countermanded, but, on the contrary, has been followed and sustained by general order, No. 207. I have received no returns of such as have reported under Schenck's order, and never will.

In your letter of the 24th of September, and others, you refer, in connection with our Gettysburg captures, to "paroles not in accordance with the cartel." The phrase figures not only in your correspondence, but in the findings of your courts and in some of your general orders. Let me here, in the most formal manner, assure you that the Confederate Government considers the cartel to be binding and imperative to the fullest extent of any and all of its provisions. I have never asked you to respect a parole which is inconsistent with that instrument. You say the Gettysburg paroles are in contravention of the cartel. Let me give you some of them—all, or nearly all, of them belong to one or the other class:

"I, the subscriber, a prisoner of war, captured near Gettysburg, Pa., do give my parole of honor not to take up arms against the Confederate States, or to do any military duty whatever, or to give any information that may be prejudicial to the interest of the same, until regularly exchanged. In the event this parole is not recognized by the Federal authorities, I give my parole of honor to report to Richmond, Va., as a prisoner of war within thirty days.

"JOHN E. PARSONS,
"1st Lieut. and Adj't. 149th Pa. Vols."

"I, the subscriber, a prisoner of war, captured near Gettysburg, Pa., do give my parole of honor not to take up arms against the Confederate States, or to do any military duty whatever, or to give any information that may be prejudicial to the interests of the same, until regularly exchanged. This parole is unconditional, and extended to a wounded officer for the sake of humanity, to save a painful and tedious journey to the rear.

"ROY STONE, Col. 149th P. V."

"We, the undersigned, of the company and regiment opposite our names, do solemnly swear that we will not take up arms against the Confederate States of America until regularly exchanged in accordance with cartel, even if required to do so by our Government."

"The following named prisoners, captured near Gettysburg, Pa., are paroled on the following conditions, namely, not to take up arms against the Confederate States, or to do any military duty whatever, or to give any information that may be prejudicial to the same, until regularly exchanged; this parole is unconditional, and if not recognized by the authorities of the United States Government, all pledge themselves to repair to Richmond, as prisoners of war, at the expiration of twenty days from this date."

Does the cartel contemplate that these officers and men should be returned to duty without exchange? It nowhere says so upon its face. When we were without any cartel, all such paroles, and, in fact, all military paroles, were respected. The very first act of the agents of exchange was to adjust mutual accounts as to the officers and men who had been captured and paroled before the cartel was signed. If it had been intended by the cartel to repudiate such paroles as were given at Gettysburg, or upon any battle field, a provision to that effect, in distinct terms, would have been incorporated in it. That instrument was intended to apply to "all prisoners of war held by either party"—to such as were in military depots or prisons, to such as had been removed from the battle field or place of capture, and reduced into actual possession. It left the force and effect of military paroles, and the respect which should be paid to them, to be determined by the usages of civilized nations of modern times. It certainly did not purpose to prevent a wounded officer or man from entering into a stipulation not to take up arms until exchanged, as the condition of his release, when his life would be at the serious risk of forfeit if he did not make the contract. Nor does it any where deny the right of any soldier, wounded or not, to bind his Government, by his military obligation, when he is in the hands of the enemy. The latter part of article seven does not really controvert this view. That clause intended to give " the commanders of two opposing armies" the power of declaring an exchange of prisoners, with the further right of paroling whatever surplus there might be after the exchange was arranged. Without such clause, the two commanders would have no right to declare an exchange. It was, therefore, inserted. Until recently, nobody ever pretended that the cartel forbid the giving and receiving of ordinary military paroles. The uniform practice under the cartel for nearly a year sanctioned them. Whatever, however, may be the determination as to this matter, it is entirely clear that at the time the Gettysburg paroles were given, your own military law required that if the parole was not approved the party should return to our lines. Many of the paroles indicate on their face that the persons giving them were aware of that fact. I have, therefore, demanded that if you reject these paroles, the parties who gave them should be returned to us. The question between us is not so much whether you will regard these paroles as valid, as whether you will comply with a rule of your own making, and which was advertised to us as being the controlling law of the case.

I know not what you mean by your reference, on your third page, to article four, of the cartel. All the officers and men whom I declared exchanged, were " actually restored to our lines." All the officers and men whom I requested you to select as equivalents for them in the exchange, " had been restored to your lines."

The parties whom I have declared exchanged, have not been " returned to their paroles, as requested by Lieut. Col. Ludlow." I do not understand by what sort of reading of the exchange notice of the 12th of September you make out that only "two officers (Generals Stevenson and Bowen)" were exchanged. My letters of July 13, September 11, and September 26, will inform you of all the Vicksburg prisoners, officers and men, whom I have declared exchanged.

Your objection to the declaration of the exchange of the general officers paroled at Vicksburg, because there were no equivalents of the same grade, is exploded by the provision of the cartel which declares that " men and officers of lower grades may be exchanged for officers of a higher grade."

I have thus answered all the items of your letter of the 24th Sept. I regret the extreme length of the reply. I have, however, confined myself to the matter of that letter, and to such subjects as were directly connected with its contents. In a future communication I will call to your attention the instances of the violation of the cartel by the Federal authorities. Notwithstanding the expression of their sudden regard for that instrument, I will show they have continued those violations from its date to the present moment.

I now inform you, in view of the recent declaration of exchange made by you, coupled with your failure either to agree to or decline the proposition made to you on the 24th of August last, in relation to paroles, that the Confederate authorities will consider themselves entirely at liberty to pursue any course as to exchange or paroles which they may deem right and proper under all the circumstances of the case. At the same time, I am directed to express their entire willingness to adopt any fair, just and reciprocal rule in relation to those subjects, without any delay.

Respectfully, your obedient servant,
ROBT. OULD,
Agent of Exchange.

[No. 28.]

BRIG. GEN. MEREDITH TO MR. OULD.

HEADQUARTERS DEP'T OF VA., 7TH ARMY CORPS,
Fort Monroe, Va., Sept. 14, 1863.

Hon. ROBERT OULD,
Agent of Exchange:

SIR: In your letter of Sept. 7th, declining to exchange General Graham for General Smith, you state "that I appear to be laboring under some strange mistake; that General Smith has already been exchanged, and, that I have received the equivalent." On July 14th, 1863, my predecessor, Lieut. Col. Ludlow, wrote to you, positively declining to unite with you in your declaration of exchange of July 13th, and requesting you to notify the officers therein named, that their exchange would not be recognized by the authorities of the United States. May I ask, who was the "equivalent" delivered for General Smith? I now repeat to you the notification of Lieut. Col. Ludlow, and state that the authorities of the United States will not recognize the exchange of the above officers until united in by me.

Respectfully, your obedient servant,
S. A. MEREDITH,
Brig. Gen. and Com'r for Exchange.

[No. 29.]

MR. OULD TO BRIG. GEN. MEREDITH.

C. S. A., War Department,
Richmond, Va., Sept. 14. 1863.

Brig. Gen. S. A. Meredith,
    Agent of Exchange:

Sir: In your letter of the 14th instant, you inquire "who was the equivalent delivered for General Smith." If you will refer to my letters of the 13th and 17th of July, you will find out who was the equivalent. It had been our practice, whenever a special exchange was declared by one party, to allow the other to select the equivalent from prisoners already paroled or delivered. I pursued that course in the case of the Vicksburg general officers. The equivalent could be found in officers and men paroled at Fredericksburg, in pursuance of an agreement between Generals Lee and Hooker. If that was not satisfactory, the equivalent could easily be found in the ten thousand prisoners whom I had released from captivity and sent to City Point. In that ten thousand there was an excess of more than six thousand, at least, over the number you had delivered at the same place since the last general declaration of exchange. My letter of the 17th of July contains a fair statement, not only of the practice of the agents of exchange, but of the grounds of my authority to declare the exchange of the Vicksburg general officers, including Gen. M. L. Smith. The effort to cast discredit upon the regular and honorable exchange of these officers, is, to use a phrase of your own, in one of your letters of the 14th instant, "simply ridiculous."

    Respectfully, your obedient servant,
        ROBERT OULD,
        Agent of Exchange.

[No. 30.]

EXCHANGE NOTICE No. 7.

Richmond, Oct. 16th, 1863.

The following Confederate officers and men are hereby declared duly exchanged:

1. All officers and men captured and paroled at any time previous to the first of September, 1863. This section, however, is not intended to include any officers or men captured at Vicksburg, July 4th, 1863, except such as were declared exchanged by exchange notice No. 6, Sept. 12th, 1863, or are specifically named in this notice. But it does embrace all deliveries made at City Point or

other place before Sept. 1st, 1863, and with the limitation above-named, all captures at Port Hudson or any other place, where the parties were released on parole.

2. The staff of Generals Pemberton, Stevenson, Bowen, Moore, Barton, S. D. Lee, Cummings, Harris, and Baldwin, and of Colonels Reynolds, Cockrell, and Dockery, the officers and men belonging to the engineer corps and sappers and miners, and the fourth and forty-sixth Mississippi regiments, all captured at Vicksburg, July 4th, 1863.

3. The general officers captured at Vicksburg, July 4th, 1863, were declared exchanged July 13th, 1863.

ROBERT OULD,
Agent of Exchange.

[No. 31.]

MR. OULD TO BRIG. GEN. MEREDITH.

Richmond, Oct. 16th, 1863.

Brig. Gen. S. A. Meredith,
Agent of Exchange:

Sir: I herewith enclose to you a declaration of exchange, which I shall publish in a day or two. You will perceive it is based upon the declaration of exchange communicated to me in your letter of the 24th of September last. In my notice I have followed your phraseology. I would have preferred another form of declaration more in accordance with the circumstances of the case. Inasmuch however, as my declaration to a considerable extent is retaliatory of yours, I have deemed it more appropriate to follow your own form of expression.

I have refrained from declaring exchanged the large residue of the Vicksburg capture. The only addition I have made to the notifications already given you as far as that capture is concerned, is the fourth and forty-sixth Mississippi regiments. According to my computation, you are considerably in debt to me upon your exchange notice, even if I take into consideration only such paroles as those to which no objection has been made. I have adopted the principles of your general orders in the computation of the paroles in my possession, and will continue to do so, until some other agreement is made between us. I reserve to myself the right to make further declarations of exchange from time to time, based upon the paroles in my office, until I have declared exchanged a number of Confederate soldiers equal to that of Federal troops declared exchanged by your last notice. At the same time, I express my entire willingness to adopt any fair, just, and reciprocal rule of computation and apply the same both to the past and the future.

Respectfully, your obedient servant,
ROBERT OULD,
Agent of Exchange.

[No. 32.]

BRIG. GEN. MEREDITH TO MR. OULD.

HEAD QUARTERS, DEPARTMEMT OF VA. AND N. C.
Fort Monroe, Oct. 17, 1862.

Hon. ROBT. OULD,
  Agent of Exchange, Richmond, Va:

SIR: On the 22d day of May, 1863, Lieut. Col. Ludlow, then agent of exchange for the United States, enclosed you copies of general orders, No. 49 and No. 100, of War Department, announcing regulations and instructions for the government of United States forces in the field, in the matter of paroles, stating that these orders and the cartel are to govern our forces; when the cartel conflicts with the orders they must be set aside. The cartel requires that prisoners of war shall be delivered at certain named places, and if they are not so delivered, the paroles cannot be valid. In consequence of the usage which had governed both parties up to that time, instructions were subsequently issued that paroles given before the 22d of May should be considered valid, though deliveries had not been made as required by the cartel. In order to the putting in force these instructions, it was not necessary to ask your consent. We were only bound to notify you that from that time the cartel would be ridgidly adhered to by us, and the same course would be exacted of the Confederate authorities.

If you wish paroles recognized when the parties were not delivered at the places named in the cartel, you "ask that paroles not in conformity with the stipulations of the cartel should be regarded as valid."

I will now proceed to show that your declaration of September 12th was not in accordance with the cartel. Your reference to acts of Lieut. Col. Ludlow does not sustain you, for, according to your own letter, Lieut. Col. L. was declaring an exchange to cover a "balance due" on declarations previously made by you. The troops thus declared exchanged by Lieut. Col. Ludlow are as follows:

51st Reg't Ind. Vol.	- - -	371
75th " " "	- - -	268
3d " Ohio "	- - -	311
Tenn. Cavalry,	- - -	58
		1,008
Poroled at Mt. Sterling,	- - -	463
		1,471

You state that the "excess," without taking into account the Mount Sterling captures, was 2,290, whereas the whole number, including said captures, amount only to 1,471.

If, in making up this balance, Lieutenent Colonel Ludlow failed to give rolls and numbers, it does not justify you in anticipating a decla ration by me, without furnishing me either rolls or numbers, or giving me time to consult the records to make them up for myself. When the paroling is properly done, both parties have rolls, and then there can be little difficulty in arranging an exchange, to be simultaneously declared. You state that when the Federal troops were declared exchanged to the 6th of May, the Confederates were declared exchanged to the 22d of May, inclusive I have nothing to show that the exchanges on both sides were not alike. The Confederate prisoners delivered between the two dates amount to 5,083 privates, and, if we have already received equivalents for them, they should be deducted from my former computation. Without counting these, the number covered by your declaration of September 12, and the subsequent explanatory declaration of September 26, amounts to 29,454.

The number of Federal troops on parole to September 1st, and declared exchanged, amounts to 23,911. The officers included are those paroled at Gettysburg and elsewhere, not those delivered at City Point.

These numbers differ from those given to you before, because, in making up that calculation, all enlisted men were counted alike, whereas non-commissioned officers should have been counted as two privates.

Giving you, then, credit for the 5,083 enlisted men, which you state were delivered at City Point between the 6th and the 23d of May, and declared exchanged by Colonel Ludlow, you are now in our debt 5,539 enlisted men.

You state that you have in your possession valid paroles, amounting to 16,000 men. For all the prisoners that we claim as on parole, we can show the rolls of delivery at the places named in the cartel, receipted by confederate officers; and if you can show similar rolls of the 16,000 men you speak of, they will, of course, be recognized as valid, and you will be credited with them.

Respectfully, your ob't servant.
S. A. MEREDITH,
Brig. Gen. an! Com. for Exch.

[No. 33.]

MR. OULD TO BRIG. GEN. MEREDITH.

RICHMOND, October 27, 1863.

Brigadier General S. A. MEREDITH,
Agent of Exchange:

SIR: In reply to your communication of the 17th instant, I state that general orders, Nos. 49 and 100 were not sent to me at the same time. I received general orders, No. 49 long before No. 100 was delivered to me. Their respective dates will show that to be the fact.

My own personal recollection is that general orders, No. 100 was never communicated in a letter. It is my habit faithfully to keep all letters written by the Federal Agent of Exchange. A careful search of the records of my office does not disclose any letter from Lieut. Col. Ludlow communicating general orders, No. 100. Lieutenant Colonel Ludlow met me at City Point on the 23d of May, 1863, and he then and there delivered to me generals orders, No. 100, stating that the principles therein announced would, in the future, control the operations of the forces of the United States. No written communication accompanied it. If any one was ever written to accompany it, I never received it. You are in error, therefore, when you say that Lieutenant Colonel Ludlow, on the 22d May, 1863, enclosed copies of general orders, No. 49 and No. 100, announcing regulations and instructions for the government of the United States forces in the field, in the matter of paroles, stating that these orders and the cartel were to govern your forces, and that when the cartel conflicted with the orders, they were to be set aside. Independent of the facts of the case, I am justified in saying that any such communication would have been very extraordinary. It would not only have admitted that the general orders were in violation of the cartel, but would have declared that the later general order, which, on its face, was announced to be the controlling law, should be set aside by the provisions contained in an earlier paper.

I again assert that the only notification I ever received as to your successive changes of purpose in the matter of paroles, was from your own general orders, according to their respective dates, delivered to me without any further comment than I have already communicated to you.

You say my "reference to the acts of Lieutenant Colonel Ludlow" does not sustain me. You further say "the troops thus declared exchanged by Lieutenant Colonel Ludlow are as follows:"

51st Regiment Indiana Volunteers,	-	-	-	-	-	71
75th " " "	-	-	-	-	-	268
2d " Ohio "	-	-	-	-	-	311
Tennessee Cavalry,	-	-	-	-	-	58
						1,008
Paroled at Mount Sterling,	-	-	-	-	-	463
						1,471

Permit me to say that I read this paragraph of your letter with very great surprise. In my letter of the 2d instant, which you were contesting, I gave, at length, the communication of Lieutenant Colonel Ludlow, and by reference to it, you will find that not only are the regiments which you have named therein mentioned, but also the Holly Springs capture, numbering 1,383 privates, the 91st Illinois regiment, numbering 649 privates, the officers and men of the Indianola, numbering 69 privates, and the 80th regiment Illinois volunteers, numbering 400 privates. Not only is that the case, but your enumeration of 1,471 privates in the specified regiments is incorrect. The true aggregate is 1,676 privates. You misname one of the regiments also. The regiment declared exchanged was not the 75th Indiana, but the 73d.

In an interview with me at City Point, in the presence of Major Mulford, you admitted that all Confederate officers and soldiers delivered at City Point before the 23d of May, 1863, were declared exchanged, while the Federal soldiers were only declared exchanged up to May 6th, 1863. Yet, in your letter written subsequent to this admission, you say you "have nothing to show that exchanges on both sides were not alike." Since your letter of the 17th, in our last interview you made the same admission. If the fact is denied at any time, I stand prepared to prove it.

As to your computation based upon my declarations of exchange, I refer you to my letter of the 2d of October, 1863. Every statement therein contained is strictly and accurately correct. I again assert what I am ready to prove, that I have in my possession more valid paroles of your officers and men than would be an equivalent for the exchanges I have declared up to this date.

Respectfully, your obedient servant,
ROBERT OULD,
Agent of Exchange.

[No. 34.]

MR. OULD TO BRIG. GEN. MEREDITH.

RICHMOND, Oct. 20, 1863.

Brig. Gen. S. A. MEREDITH,
Agent of Exchange:

SIR: More than a month ago I asked your acquiescence in a proposition, that all officers and soldiers on both sides should be released in conformity with the provisions of the cartel. In order to obviate the difficulties between us, I suggested that all officers and men on both sides should be released, unless they were subject to charges; in which event, the opposite Government should have the right of holding one or more hostages, if the retention was not justified. You stated to me, in conversation, that this proposition was very fair, and that you would ask the consent of your Government to it. As usual, you have as yet made no response. I tell you frankly, I do not expect any. Perhaps you may disappoint me, and tell me that you reject or accept the proposition. I write this letter for the purpose of bringing to your recollection my proposition, and of dissipating the idea that seems to have been purposely encouraged by your public papers, that the Confederate Government has refused or objected to a system of exchanges.

In order to avoid any mistake in that direction, I now propose that all officers and men on both sides be released in conformity with the provisions of the cartel, the excess on one side or the other to be on parole. Will you accept this? I have no expectation of an answer, but perhaps you may give one. If it does come, I hope it will be soon.

    Respectfully, your obedient servant,
            ROBERT OULD,
              Agent of Exchange.

[No. 85.]

MR. OULD TO BRIG. GEN. MEREDITH.

            RICHMOND, Oct. 27th, 1863.

Brig. Gen. S. A. MEREDITH,
  Agent of Exchange:

SIR: I enclose to you a memorandum of the paroles to which I have referred in several recent communications. Most of these paroles, you will observe, are antecedent to May 23d, 1863. The reason why these paroles have not been heretofore discharged, is that up to July, 1863, we had the advantage of prisoners and paroles. Not one of these paroles is covered by any declaration of exchange, except the one lately made by you. For no one of them have I received any equivalent. All of them since the date of your general orders, No. 207, were given in pursuance of a distinct agreement between the commanders of two opposing armies. I have many other paroles in my possession, but I have only presented those which are within the terms of your general orders, according to their respective dates.

I understand there are other paroles coming within the same general orders, which were given by your officers and men on the other side of the Mississippi river. They have not as yet reached me. When they do, and when I show they are within the scope of your general orders, I will claim them—otherwise I will discard them.

I have also received other informal paroles, which I have sent back for correction. These are also within the provisions of your general orders. When they are returned, I will claim them also.

    Respectfully, your obedient servant,
            ROBERT OULD,
              Agent of Exchange.

[No. 36.]

BRIG. GEN. MEREDITH TO MR. OULD.

Office Commissioner for Exchange,
Fortress Monroe, Va., Oct. 29, 1863.

Hon. Robert Ould,
   Agent of Exchange, Richmond, Va.

Sir: I am in receipt of your communication of the 20th instant, the tenor of which induces me to make some explanatory statements of facts, with which, it would seem, you need to be reminded.

The system of exchanges, of prisoners of war, determined in the existing cartel, was first interrupted by the declared purpose of the Confederate Government to make certain distinctions in the treatment of a particular class of troops, officers and men, in violation of the provisions of the cartel. This appears to have been the first step towards the irregularities which have culminated in your unequivocal declaration, reported by me to my government on the 8th instant, that "you will proceed to declare exchanges whenever you conscientiously feel that you have the right to do so, for the purpose of putting men into the field."

There can be no objections to your acting conscientiously in any given case, so long as your conscience is enlightened and guided by those laws of war which require obedience between belligerents to solemn agreements, entered into by authorized commissioners acting in the name of their respective superiors. But, if you mean by the expression, "your conscientious sense of right," to substitute this sense of right for the requirements of an existing cartel, I can by no means concede to you that right; and if you do not mean this, I cannot understand what you do mean by so vague and general a declaration. Judging by your recent proceedings, it seems that you have declared exchanged all Confederate officers and soldiers on parole within what you claim as your lines, up to a very recent date, without having any proper right so to do, either under the cartel or under the laws of war.

The history of this matter, as I understand it, is briefly this: While my predecessor, on duty at this place, was here, in discharge of the duties now committed to me, you at one time made a declaration of exchange, embracing no great number of prisoners of war, not in accordance with the requirements of the cartel, and you invited Col. Ludlow, my predecessor, to make a corresponding declaration of equivalents. Such a declaration was made by Col. Ludlow, doubtless without anticipating the magnitude of the evil which appears now as the result of that departure from the cartel, first inaugurated by yourself. Subsequently to my coming on duty here, the events of the war threw upon your hands a large body of paroled officers and men (over 30,000,) captured by General Grant at Vicksburg, and not long afterwards some 6,000 or more captured by General Banks at Port Hudson.

Suddenly, and without any proper conference or understanding with ice, and but a few days prior to the important events at Chickamauga, as if for the express purpose of increasing the force of General Bragg against General Rosencrans, you gave me notice that, on the next day after the date of that notice, you would declare exchanged a large portion of the troops which had been captured by Gen'l Grant.

When your declaration was made, it covered an indeterminate number of troops, designated by commands, brigades, divisions and corps, no definite number either of officers or men being designated. Up to that time, you had delivered at City Point a certain number of prisoners of war, for which you had receipts, by which you must have known the number you might claim the right to discharge from their parole. You did not think proper to limit yourself to this number, nor, in any proper manner did you refer to it, but made your declaration of exchange in such indefinite terms as made it next to certain that you did not intend to be governed by the cartel.

On referring to the data furnished by the reports of General Grant, and now in the hands of the Commissary General of prisoners at Washington, it was ascertained that you had discharged from parole, by your declaration, a very considerable number of your men over and above any claim you might pretend to, founded on receipts for prisoners of war delivered from the South according to the cartel.

Without referring to fractions, it appeared, from the best data in our hands, that you had discharged *three* for *two*, or one-third more than you were entitled to.

You suggested that I should make a corresponding declaration of exchange, when, as I suppose, you must have known you had not delivered to me, nor had you valid paroles of our men sufficient to cover the number declared exchanged by yourself; and, when I proceeded to make the declaration extending to those men you had delivered, and stated to you my objection to your proceedings, you insisted that you had valid paroles for more than the number that you had declared exchanged, though you failed to produce those paroles, or to give any account or history of them ; and you then proceeded to make a further declaration of exchange, ignoring the cartel altogether—basing your action upon no data communicated to me, the whole proceeding resting, as I suppose you will say, upon *your* sense of right, as if you were the only party having a *right* to an opinion on the subject—acting evidently in anticipation of the formal declaration referred to at the commencement of this communication, "that you will proceed to make declarations of exchange for the purpose of putting troops into the field, whenever you think proper;" and, having now exhausted, by a declaration of exchange, the paroled prisoners in your hands, you propose to me the delivery of prisoners of war in our hands, for whom you have no equivalents—or, comparatively, but very few—in order, as it were, that you may obtain possession of many thousand more men of your own, delivered or on parole, for the purpose of declaring them also exchanged, and putting them into the field, not in conformity with the existing cartel, nor in accordance with the usages of war, but whenever, in your individual judgment, you may think it proper to do so.

I have only to add, that an easy inference from this statement is the answer I have to make to your proposal of the 20th instant, which is not accepted.

Respectfully, your obedient servant,
S. A. MEREDITH,
Brig. Gen. and Commissioner for Exchange.

[No. 37]

MR. OULD TO BRIG. GEN. MEREDITH.

CONFEDERATE STATES OF AMERICA, WAR DEPARTMENT,
Richmond, October 31, 1863.

Brig. Gen. S. A. MEREDITH,
Agent of Exchange:

SIR: Your communication of the 29th instant, has been received, and its extraordinary and groundless statements read with surprise.

You first represent me as having informed you that I would proceed to declare exchanges whenever I conscientiously felt that I had the right to do so, for the purpose of putting men into the field. In another part of your letter I am charged with having stated that I would proceed to make declarations of exchange for the purpose of putting troops into the field, whenever I thought proper. Both of these paragraphs are between quotation marks, to indicate that I had communicated them. Moreover, they are mentioned as being my "unequivocal declaration." Upon a faithful examination of my correspondence with you and your predecessor, I can find no instance in which such language has been used by me. Will you inform me of the date of any such communication, or furnish me with a copy of it? If you cannot, you will certainly deem me justified in denouncing your statement as utterly without foundation in truth.

Upon these premises you have proceeded to throw off sundry sentences, more flippant than worthy of notice. As usual, however, you finish the paragraph which contains them with a misstatement, in asserting that I "have declared exchanged all Confederate officers and men on parole," within our lines, "up to a very recent date." I have done no such thing. I specially excepted the larger part of the Vicksburg captures.

You then proceed to give what you call "a history of this matter." That history, like many others, turns out to be a romance. Lieut. Col. Ludlow's declarations of exchange, to which I referred in my letter of October 2, 1863, were not made in response to any invitation from me, or in consequence of any previous declarations which I had made. I did not "inaugurate" what you term "a departure from the cartel." The correspondence of the office very clearly shows that fact.

You are wrong, also, in your statement that the Vicksburg capture was subsequent to your "coming to duty" at Fortress Monroe. I received official communications from Lieut. Col. Ludlow as late as July 22, 1863, weeks after the Vicksburg surrender, and none from you until the 25th of the same month.

Your charge that the declaration of exchange, bearing date September 12, 1863, was made "as if for the express purpose of increasing the force of General Bragg against General Rosencrans." This, also, is untrue. The declaration was not published until several days after the 12th, although it bore that date. Not one of the officers or men named in that declaration of exchange was on the battle-field of Chickamauga.

You further say I must have known that I had not delivered to you, nor had I valid paroles of your men, sufficient to cover the number declared exchanged by me. I knew exactly the contrary, and so informed you. On the 12th of September, 1863, in announcing the declaration of exchange I would make on the following day, I wrote to you that I had "in my possession more valid paroles of your officers and men than would be an equivalent for the officers and men" enumerated in the exchange notice. I have made the same statement to you more than once since. I am prepared to prove that it was true each time it was uttered.

You say your declaration of exchange extended to those whom I had *delivered*. If you mean that it was limited to such, you are incorrect; for it declared exchanged all officers and men of the United States army captured and paroled at any time previous to the 1st of September, 1863, and included many thousands of prisoners taken and paroled by our cavalry and other forces, in many States of the Confederacy, never delivered by me. I have already furnished you a memorandum of at least sixteen thousand of these paroled prisoners.

You say I failed to produce the paroles, or to give any account or history of them. If you mean that I refused to do so, it is not true. I offered to produce them at any time, and importuned you to agree to some principle by which they could be computed and adjusted. When I last met you at City Point, you requested me for the first time to send to you a memorandum of the paroles claimed as valid by me. I furnished you with the list on the 27th instant, that being the first day, after your request, on which a flag of truce boat appeared at City Point.

You say I then proceeded to make a further declaration of exchange, ignoring the cartel altogether, and resting the whole proceeding, as you suppose, on my sense of right. There, again, you are mistaken. I did not rest the proceeding entirely upon my sense of right; I relied, in some measure, upon yours, and to that extent, its propriety may be doubtful. In communicating to you Exchange Notice, No. 7, which is the one to which you refer, I wrote to you as follows: "I herewith enclose to you a declaration of exchange, which I shall publish in a day or two. You will perceive it is based upon the declaration of exchange communicated to me in your letter of the 24th of September last. In my notice I have followed your phraseology. I would have preferred another form of declaration, more in accordance with the circumstances of the case. Inasmuch, however, as my declaration, to a considerable extent, is retaliatory of yours, I have deemed it more appropriate to follow your own form of expression." Your letter of the 24th of September declared that "all officers and men of the United States army, captured and paroled at any time previous to the 1st of September, 1863, are duly exchanged." On the 16th of October following, I declared exchanged "all [Confederate] officers and men captured and paroled at any time previous to the 1st of September, 1863." If that was "ignoring the cartel," as you charge. I only followed your example. Our declarations of exchange were precisely similar, except that in another part of my notice I reserved from its operation the larger part of the Vicksburg paroles. If I had followed your "sense of right," as I then had and still claim the right to do, I would have included all.

The Confederate authorities take it unto themselves as a proud and honorable boast, that they have determined all these matters of paroles and exchanges according to their "sense of right," and not by any views of temporary expediency. In following that guide, they have at least shunned some examples furnished by your Government. They have never, in violation of their general orders, and without notice to the adverse party, ordered their paroled officers and men to break their solemn covenant, and, without exchange, lift their arms against their captors. They have, therefore, escaped the pangs of that retributive justice which made your general order of July 3, 1863, though so well suited to the meridian of Gettysburg, invalidate the paroles given at Port Hudson, on the 9th of the same month. Upon further reflection, I am sure you will be satisfied that it does not become your authorities, who have chosen, whenever they felt so disposed, without notice or consent from us, to repudiate the established usages of exchange, and put new constructions upon the cartel, to complain that others have acted according to their sense of right.

Not content with all the misstatements of fact which I have cited, you have, in your letter of the 29th instant, descended to a malignant and wanton aspersion of the motives of the Confederate authorities in making the proposal contained in my letter of the 20th instant. You were asked to agree "that all officers and men on both sides should be released, the excess on one side or the other to be on parole." It would have been injustice enough to the many thousands of your prisoners in our hands, and to those of ours in your custody, simply to have declined the proposal. But you have thought proper to add to your refusal the gratuitous insult to the Confederate States, of intimating that their fair and honest offer was made for the purpose of putting into the field officers and men fraudulently exchanged. This calumny is as destitute of foundation in fact, as it is despicable in spirit.

In conclusion, let me tell you that the purpose of your letter is apparent. It has been well known for a long time that your authorities are opposed to a fair and regular exchange of prisoners under the cartel. In rejecting my proposition you have endeavored to conceal, under a cloud of vague charges and unfounded statements, the determination at which your Government long since arrived. Why not be frank once? Why not say, without any further subterfuges, that you have reached the conclusion that our officers and soldiers are more valuable, man for man, than yours?

Respectfully, your obedient servant,

RO. OULD, *Agent of Exchange.*

[No. 38.]

BRIG. GEN. MEREDITH TO MR. OULD.

OFFICE OF COMMISSIONER FOR EXCHANGE, }
Fortress Monroe, Va., Nov. 7th, 1863. }

Hon ROBERT OULD,
Agent of Exchange, Richmond, Va.:

SIR: In your communication of Oct. 27th, you state, "that general orders Nos. 49 and 100 were not sent to you at the same time." I forward you herewith a copy of Lieut. Col. Ludlow's letter, inclosing to you the two orders above-mentioned, and bearing date May 22d, 1863.

These two orders announced general rules, based on the usages of war, which, in the absence of any specific agreement between belligerents, should govern in paroling prisoners of war, but in this case, a cartel had already been agreed upon, and no order of either party could set aside any of its provisions. For instance: A commander, on being captured, might, under some circumstances, give a parole for himself and his command, without violating general order No. 100, (which includes general order No. 49,) but unless the paroling was done at City Point or other named place, it would be in violation of the cartel, and the paroles must therefore be set aside as invalid. No exception could be taken to this course by the party granting the parole, because the validity of the parole depends on a strict compliance with the provisions of the cartel, and when any other course is followed, than that pointed out by that instrument, any claim based upon it must fail. Paragraph 130, of order 100, which prescribes the duties which a paroled soldier may perform, is also, to some extent, set aside by the cartel, which restricts these duties to a much more limited field than the order. Paragraph 131 is also made inoperative by the cartel, because it could only apply to paroles not given at the points designated for delivery; all such paroles are, by the cartel, made invalid, and the paroling party could therefore have no pretext for claiming their recognition. If such a claim could be admitted, the effect at Gettysburg would have been to give to Gen. Lee, the privilege of placing his prisoners in our hands, to be delivered to him, at our own charge, at City Point, which is so manifestly absurd, that even you cannot claim it. General order No. 207, was intended simply to announce to the army, that the irregular practice of paroling small squads of men and individuals, without rolls or other reliable evidence of any kind, which had very generally prevailed, must be discontinued, and that thereafter, the cartel should be rigidly adhered to. This announcement had been made to the Confederate authorities through you.

There have been no "successive changes of purpose in the matter of paroles," as you assert, nor changes of any kind, except so far as to return to a strict observance of the cartel; and this is a change, the propriety of which, I do not think you can question.

The figures which I gave you in my letter of October 17th, were not given as embracing all declared exchanged in general order 167, of June 8th, but only those which Lieut. Col. Ludlow used, to make up the *balance* due him after arranging that declaration with you. It was the declaration which Lieut. Col. Ludlow made to cover this balance, that you cite, as the precedent which authorized you to announce so unexpectedly your declaration of September 12th. The 50th Illinois, 311 men, not 400, as you say, was accidentally omitted from my letter, and, by a clerical error, the 73d Indiana was written 75th Indiana. Paragraphs 5 and 6, of General Order 167, cover the troops referred to, and other paragraphs cover the captures mentioned by you. Any discrepancy in numbers declared exchanged at that time, on either side, is of little consequence, as up to the date of that order, it is assumed that the exchange account was satisfactorily balanced.

Respectfully, your obedient servant,
S. A. MEREDITH,
Brig. Gen. and Com'r for Exchange.

[No. 39.]

LIEUT. COL. LUDLOW TO MR. OULD.

HEADQUARTERS DEP'T OF VA., 7TH ARMY CORPS,
Fort Monroe, Va., May 22, 1863.

Hon. ROBERT OULD,
Agent for Exchange of Prisoners:

SIR: I have the honor to enclose to you copies of General Orders No. 49 and No. 100, of War Department, announcing regulations and instructions for the government of the United States forces in the field, in the matter of paroles. These, together with the stipulations of the cartel, will govern our army. I would invite your special attention to article 7 of the cartel, which provides that all prisoners of war shall be sent to places of delivery therein specified. The execution of this article will obviate much discussion and difficulty growing out of the mode, time, and place of giving paroles. No paroles or exchanges will be considered binding, except those under the stipulations of said article, permitting commanders of two opposing armies to exchange or release on parole at other points mutually agreed on by said commanders.

I am, very respectfully,
Your obedient servant,
WM. H. LUDLOW,
Lieut. Col. and Agent for Exchange of Prisoners.

[No. 40.]

MR. OULD TO BRIG. GEN. MEREDITH.

C. S. A., WAR DEPARTMENT,
Richmond, Va., Nov. 18th, 1863.

Brig. Gen. S. A. MEREDITH,
Agent of Exchange:

SIR: In your communication of Nov. 7th, 1863, you enclose a copy of a letter bearing date May 22d, 1863, purporting to have been written by Lieut. Col. Ludlow and addressed to me.

I reiterate what I have before said, that general order No. 100, when it was delivered to me, was not accompanied by any written communication. You are aware that Lieut. Col. Ludlow was at City Point on the 23d of May. It is unquestionably true that he wrote the aforesaid letter on the 22d, at Fortress Monroe. It is just as true that he brought it with him to City Point. My own personal recollection is perfectly distinct that, at the conclusion of our interview at City Point, he took the pamphlet containing general order No. 100 from a package, the seal of which he broke at the time, and delivered said order into my hands, with the remark that its provisions in the future would govern the operations of the United States forces. Why he retained the letter I do not know. The fact, however, is exactly as I have stated it, and fully explains why a copy of the letter was on Lieut. Col. Ludlow's letter book. I do not want to be understood for one moment as imputing any fraud or improper conduct in what Lieut. Col. Ludlow did in the premises. He undoubtedly thought the remark he made at the time of the delivery dispensed with the necessity of giving me the letter.

Respectfully, your obedient servant,
ROBERT OULD,
Agent of Exchange.

CORRESPONDENCE

Relative to General Morgan and his men.

[No. 41.]

BRIG. GEN. MEREDITH TO MR. OULD.

OFFICE COMMISSIONER FOR EXCHANGE,
Fortress Monroe, July 30, 1863.

Hon. ROBERT OULD,
    Commissioner for Exchange, &c., Richmond, Va.:

SIR: This will inform you, and, through you, the authorities under whom you act, that General John H. Morgan and his officers will be placed in close confinement and held as hostages for the members of Colonel Streight's command, who have not been delivered in compliance with the conditions of the cartel agreed to by Major General Dix and Major General Hill.

    Respectfully, your obedient servant,
        S. A. MEREDITH,
    Brig. Gen. U. S. Vols. and Com'r for Exchange.

[No. 42.]

MR. OULD TO BRIG. GEN. MEREDITH.

WAR DEPARTMENT,
Richmond, Va., August 1, 1863.

Brigadier General S. A. MEREDITH,
    Agent of Exchange:

SIR: I am in receipt of your communication of the 30th ultimo, informing me that "General John H. Morgan and his officers will be placed in close confinement and held as hostages for the members of Colonel Streight's command." I beg leave respectfully to ask what you mean by "close confinement?" In what respect will that "close confinement" differ from the confinement of other prisoners, officers and men.

Colonel Streight's command is treated exactly as are the other officers held in captivity by us. What that treatment is you can find from any conscientious officer who has lately been confined in the Libby. You will hear no complaint from me or from the Confederate authorities so long as our officers receive the treatment which yours do here.

You further say that "Colonel Streight's command have not been delivered in compliance with the conditions of the cartel agreed to by Major General Dix and Major General Hill.

In retaining Colonel Streight and his command the Confederate authorities have not gone as far as those of the United States have claimed for themselves the right to go ever since the establishment of that cartel. You have claimed and exercised the right to retain officers and men indefinitely, not only upon charges actually preferred, but upon mere suspicions. You have now in custody officers who were in confinement when the cartel was framed, and who have since been declared exchanged. Some of them have been tried, but most of them have languished in prison all the weary time without trial or charges. I stand prepared to prove these assertions. This course was pursued, too, in the face not only of notice but protest. Do you deny us the right to detain officers and men for trial upon grave charges, while you claim the right to keep in confinement any who may be the objects of your suspicion or special enmity?

Respectfully, your obedient servant,
ROBERT OULD,
Agent of Exchange.

[No. 43.]

MR. OULD TO BRIG. GEN. MEREDITH.

RICHMOND, August 28, 1863.

Brig. Gen. S. A. MEREDITH,
Agent of Exchange:

SIR: Some time ago I addressed a communication to you, asking why you held General Morgan in close confinement, and what was its nature? To that I have received no reply. In that I am not disappointed, as it is not the habit of the Federal agent of exchange to answer enquiries. Since then I have seen in your papers detailed accounts of the treatment General Morgan and his brother officers have received. What does this mean? It is alleged that this course is pursued in retaliation for the confinement of Colonel Streight and his officers. I have already assured you that those officers are treated exactly as all others held in confinement at the Libby. Colonel Streight has expressed to me, in person, his satisfaction as to the manner in which he was treated. Do you wish him shaved and put in a felon's cell? If you do, you are pursuing exactly the course to effect it. May I again ask, why have you put General Morgan and his brother officer in a penitentiary? I have but faint hopes of getting any reply, but under the circumstances I have ventured the question.

Respectfully, your obedient servant,
ROBERT OULD,
Agent of Exchange.

[No. 44.]

BRIG. GEN. MEREDITH TO MR. OULD.

HEADQUARTERS DEPARTMENT OF VA., 7TH ARMY CORPS, *Fortress Monroe*, Sept. 30, 1863.

Hon. ROBERT OULD,

Agent of Exchange, Richmond, Va.:

SIR: Had I succeeded—after waiting thirty hours—in obtaining an interview with you when I was last at City Point—I had intended to explain to you that the United States authorities had nothing whatever to do with the treatment that General Morgan and his command received when imprisoned at Columbus. Such treatment was wholly unauthorized.

Very respectfully, your obedient servant,
S. A. MEREDITH,
Brig. Gen. and Com'r for Exchange.

[No. 45.]

MR. OULD TO BRIG. GEN. MEREDITH.

RICHMOND, October 2, 1863.

Brig. Gen. S. A. MEREDITH,

Agent of Exchange:

SIR: As you did not have the opportunity to explain to me at City Point how "the United States authorities had nothing to do with the treatment that General Morgan and his command received when imprisoned at Columbus," will you be so kind as to do it now? I thought Morgan and his command were prisoners of war, captured by the United States forces, and therefore in their custody. You and I have talked twice about General Morgan, and no hint was thrown out that he was not a prisoner of the United States. So far from that, on the

30th of July last, you informed me by letter that "General John H. Morgan and his officers will be placed in close confinement and held as hostages for the members of Colonel Streight's command." Will you please explain to me what you meant by this notice of the 30th of July, if "the United States authorities had nothing to do with the treatment that General Morgan and his command received." Nay, more, will you enlighten me as to the point, why the United States authorities have allowed their prisoners and "hostages" to receive such "unauthorized treatment" for two months? I hope the reason is not of such a nature that it can only be communicated in a whisper. Let me have it on paper.

Respectfully, your obedient servant,
ROBERT OULD,
Agent of Exchange.

[No. 46.]

MR. OULD TO BRIG. GEN. MEREDITH.

RICHMOND, October 13, 1863.

Brig. Gen. S. A. MEREDITH,
Agent of Exchange:

SIR: Accompanying this communication you will find the copy of a letter from Lieutenant Colonel Alston, of General Morgan's command. Lieutenant Colonel Alston is the officer who was delivered at City Point by the last flag of true boat. On the 30th of September last, you informed me that "the United States authorities had nothing whatever to do with the treatment that General Morgan and his command received when imprisoned at Columbus." In my interview with you, about one week ago, you informed me that General Morgan and his officers were held for others than "the members of Colonel Streight's command." You showed me a letter from General Hitchcock, in which the fact was announced. It seems that your authorities, having been assured, either from my representations or from those of your own people in confinement at Richmond, that Colonel Streight and his officers were receiving precisely the same treatment as that of other prisoners, they have adopted some other excuse for the continued confinement of General Morgan and his officers in a penitentiary. I ask if this does not show a determination to keep these officers in a confinement intended to be ignominious? When one excuse fails another is set up.

Your Secretary of War has himself borne testimony of the "honor" of Lieutenant Colonel Alston. I therefore call your attention to his communication, and again ask you how can General Morgan's original incarceration in the Ohio penitentiary, his continued confinement therein, the indignities received by him and his brother officers, and your announcement at our last interview be explained, if "the United

States authorities had nothing to do with the treatment General Morgan and his command received when imprisoned at Columbus?" Will you also inform me whether the "United States authorities" intend to treat these officers as felons in the future? And, if not, whether those authorities will allow others so to treat them?

Respectfully, your obedient servant,
RO. OULD,
Agent of Exchange

[No. 47.]

LIEUT. COL. ALSTON TO MR. SEDDON.

Richmond, October 10, 1863.

Hon. James A. Seddon,
  Secretary of War:

In compliance with your request, I beg leave to submit the following statement:

On the 5th day of July last, Brigadier General John H. Morgan, in command of a force of Confederate cavalry, attacked the Federal garrison at Lebanon, Kentucky, which consisted of the twentieth regiment Kentucky volunteer infantry, about five hundred men, and a section of artillery, about forty men, all under the command of Lieut. Colonel Charles L. Hanson. After a severe engagement of about seven hours. Colonel Hanson surrendered the entire force that had not been killed. He requested General Morgan to parole him and his command, to which General Morgan objected, "that his (Colonel Hanson's) Government had published a general order, that no more such paroles would be respected." Colonel Hanson replied, "that he was aware of this order, but this was a case which he believed, on proper representation to higher authority, would be permitted as an exception to this order; and, at any rate, if General Morgan would grant the parole to himself and the officers and men of his regiment he would pledge his personal honor that he not only would observe it but would see that every other one to whom the privilege was extended should observe it. If, after making a proper statement of all the facts to higher authority, he should be ordered back into service, he would pledge himself to report to General Morgan at some point within the Confederate lines.

This interview took place in the presence of several officers, among whom were Captain Davis, Assistant Adjutant General of Duke's brigade, who was an official witness of all that was said, and who immediately reported it to me, and brought the order from General Morgan for me to parole Colonel Hanson and his men and officers. Acting under these instructions, I paroled them on the evening of the 5th of July, and on the 8th of July, Captain William Campbell, of our command, and a small detachment of his men, were captured by a portion of this very regiment, and were treated, on their arrival at

Nicholasville, with the greatest indiguity by Capt. Frank E. Walcott, of company F, of the same regiment. He not only abused the men as a parcel of horse thieves and scoundrels, but took their boots and hats from them and threw them away in their presence. Lieutenant Colonel Hanson also came up a short time afterwards, and took from one of the parties some crackers and cheese, which he had been allowed by the sergeant to purchase.

In a few days afterwards Lieutenant Colonel Hanson was ordered to Louisville to do provost duty, relieving Lieutenant Colonel Sterritt, of the twenty-fifth Michigan volunteer infantry, who was ordered to the field. He and his regiment are still on duty there.

On the 26th July, Brigadier General Morgan and most of his officers were captured. They were carried to Cincinnati, and from thence he and twenty-eight of his officers were selected and carried to Columbus, Ohio, where they were shaved and their hair cut very close by a negro convict. They were then marched to the bath room and scrubbed, and from there to their cells, where they were locked up. The Federal papers published, with great delight, a minute account of the whole proceedings. Seven days afterwards, forty-two more of General Morgan's officers were conveyed from Johnson's Island to the penitentiary, and subjected to the same indignities. I have seen Colonel D. Harrard Smith, one of the officers who was conveyed there among the second lot, and he told me that Mr. Merrion, the warden, apologized for such treatment; but he had distinctly informed General Burnside that he would receive them on no other terms, and he had sent them.

* * * * * * * * *

Very respectfully submitted by your obedient servant,

R. ALSTON,
Lieutenant Colonel P. A. C. S.

CORRESPONDENCE

Relative to the Detention of Surgeons.

[No. 48.]

MR. OULD TO LIEUT. COL. LUDLOW.

Richmond, Va., *May* 29, 1863.

Lieut. Col. Wm. H. Ludlow,
    Agent of Exchange:

Sir: The names of several Confederate officers, including that of Col. Morehead, who were long since declared exchanged under our agreements, appear upon one of your recent rolls. These officers were not delivered to us. I understand they are detained at or near Old Point. Are these officers to be delivered to us or not? One of them is a Confederate surgeon—Dr. Mead. Do you intend to retain surgeons?

There is not a single Federal officer in our custody who has been declared exchanged, unless it may be Rucker; and for him you hold Dr. Green. On what pretence are these officers held? I will be obliged to you, if you will inform me what course you intend to pursue in reference to such cases.

    Respectfully, your obedient servant,
        RO. OULD, *Agent of Exchange.*

[No. 49.]

LIUT. COL. LUDLOW TO MR. OULD.

Headquarters Department of Virginia, 7th Army Corps,
    Fort Monroe, June 9, 1863.

Hon. Robert Ould,
    Agent for Exchange of Prisoners:

Sir: Please have ready for delivery, all our officers in your hands who have been declared exchanged—Spencer Kellogg among the number. Deliveries of your officers declared exchanged can then be effected. I would suggest to you that Dr. Rucker be included. I very much desire that all surgeons should be treated as non-combatants, and unconditionally released. As I have before remarked to you, the cause of humanity demands it.

I saw Dr. Green at Fort Norfolk. He is most anxious to know what is to be his fate. Can you inform him?

I am, very respectfully,
Your obedient servant,
WM. H. LUDLOW,
Lieut. Col., and Agent for Exchange of Prisoners.

[No. 50.]

MR. OULD TO LIEUT. COL. LUDLOW.

CONFEDERATE STATES OF AMERICA, WAR DEPARTMENT,
Richmond, Va, June 12, 1863.

Lieut. Col WM. H. LUDLOW,
Agent of Exchange:

SIR: Dr. Rucker is prosecuted by the State of Virginia, for offences against her laws, for which he had no warrant in your own military law to commit. If you have any such officer of the Confederate States in any such position, even though he may have been declared exchanged by our general agreements, I cannot complain of his retention.

With this proper limitation, extending to only one case, I am ready, at any moment, to deliver you every officer or man whom we have declared exchanged. I do not believe there are any such in our prisons. I have, however, caused diligent search to be made, and if any such are discovered, they will be promptly delivered to you.

I hope, therefore, you will have all our exchanged officers and men sent to City Point immediately. You will find there any of the same class whom I can discover. I will be thankful to you for any names which you may be able to furnish. Spencer Kellogg's case is already under inquiry.

With the limitation as to Dr. Rucker, I am entirely agreed to release unconditionally all surgeons. I agree with you, that the cause of humanity demands it, unless, indeed, it is shown that the surgeon has committed offences which prove him to be a savage and a beast.

Respectfully, your obedient servant,
RO. OULD, *Agent of Exchange.*

[No. 51.]

LIEUT. COL. LUDLOW TO MR. OULD.

HEADQUARTERS DEPARTMENT OF VIRGINIA, 7TH ARMY CORPS.
Fort Monroe, June 14, 1863.

Hon. ROBERT OULD,
    Agent for Exchange :

SIR: Dr. Green will be retained as a hostage for Dr. Rucker. All other surgeons in our custody (three or four now being here) will be released and delivered to you, on the release and delivery to me of all you hold, except Dr. Rucker.

Do you agree to this, with the additional understanding that the detentions of surgeons shall be confined to these two?

Please inform me when Spencer Kellogg, and other of our officers declared exchanged, will be delivered at City Point, in order that arrangements may be made for sending up such of your exchanged officers as are at Fort Norfolk awaiting delivery.

I am, very respectfully,
    Your obedient servant,
        WM. H. LUDLOW,
    Lieut. Col., and Agent for Exchange of Prisoners.

[No. 52.]

LIEUT. COL. LUDLOW TO MR. OULD.

HEADQUARTERS DEP'T OF VA., 7TH ARMY CORPS.
Fort Monroe, June 18th, 1863.

Hon. ROBERT OULD,
    Agent for Exchange of Prisoners:

SIR: I send to you Col. Moorhead and Captain Flint, who have been declared exchanged. Also, all the Surgeons we have here, excepting Dr. Green.

Capt. Mulford is instructed to bring back Col Moorhead, unless Spencer Kellogg, declared exchanged, be delivered, if in Richmond, or if he be not, unless you give an agreement that Kellogg shall be delivered at City Point within two weeks.

Capt. Mulford is also instructed to bring back the Surgeons, unless he receives all our Surgeons now confined in Richmond, except Dr. Rucker; whom you retain under charges, and for whom Dr. Green is held as a hostage.

I am, very respectfully,
    Your obedient servant,
        WM. H. LUDLOW,
    Lieut. Col., and Agent for Exchange of Prisoners.

Among the Surgeons retained by you, are Dr. Spencer, assistant surgeon of the 73d Indiana; also, Dr. Myers, U. S. N.

W. H. L.

[No. 53.]

MR. OULD TO LIEUT. COL. LUDLOW.

CONFEDERATE STATES OF AMERICA,
War Department,
Richmond, Va., June 28d, 1863.

Lieut. Col. WM. H. LUDLOW,
  Agent of Exchange:

SIR: The grounds upon which Dr. Rucker has been retained have already been very fully communicated to you. He has been indicted by the Commonwealth of Virginia for offences committed within her limits, which are not sanctioned by any civilized military code. He was not under the protection of a soldier when he committed the felonies charged against him. The State is now prosecuting him for these crimes, and his trial has been delayed for two terms of the Court, at his own instance, as I am informed.

You have said to me that the principles announced in general order No. 100, are to apply against you as well as for you. In that order you distinctly recognize the right of an invaded State to punish all wanton violence committed against its citizens, as well as all destruction of property not commanded by the authorized officer. I refer you to paragraphs 44, 47 and especially 59. If I had the framing of a provision to meet Dr. Rucker's case and to justify his detention, I could not use apter terms than those employed in paragraph 59.

Moreover, you have claimed and exercised the right of holding many of our officers and soldiers on mere suspicion, for months, without trial or proceedings of any sort against them. You have such in confinement now. For them, we have selected none of your officers or soldiers in retaliation. Yet, when we retain the first of yours, under indictment preferred by a grand jury, you immediately select one of ours in retaliation. If we had applied any such rule to you since the beginning of the war, how many of your officers and soldiers would be now in our prisons?

I lament with you the detention of surgeons. I am willing to do anything consistent with honor and justice to promote their discharge. But we cannot surrender a clear right. Dr. Rucker's detention is justified by your own principles and practice. I have already admitted your right to detain any one of our officers under similar circumstances.

If we are justified by the rules of war in detaining for trial Dr. Rucker, what right have you to hold Dr. Green in retaliation?

Your request for the discharge of all surgeons, except Drs. Ruker and Green, is simply asking me to admit that the former is unjustly detained, and the latter rightly held in retaliation. I deny both, and appeal to your own military laws. As Dr. Rucker has asked to have his trial posponed, let his case remain as it is, and let us unconditionally release all other surgeons on both sides. If any grand jury of yours indicts any surgeon, or other officer of ours for such offences as are charged against Dr. Rucker, and he is detained for trial, I am sure I will not complain.

Respectfully, your obedient servant,

ROBERT OULD, *Agent of Exchange.*

[No. 54.]

LIEUT. COL. LUDLOW TO MR OULD.

HEADQUARTERS, DEP'T. OF VA., 7TH ARMY CORPS, }
Fort Monroe, July 12, 1863. }

Hon. ROBERT OULD,
Agent for Exchange of Prisoners.

SIR: As understood by me, Dr. Rucker's alleged offences were committed in west Virginia, within the territory militarily occupied at the time by the troops of the United States. If so, by the laws and usages of war, your authorities have no jurisdiction in his case.

If you will release all our medical officers, except Dr Rucker, I will send to you all we hold, except one, to be retained as a hostage for Dr. Rucker, who will be released when Dr. Rucker is released.

If it should be found that Dr. Rucker is properly retained under the cartel, or found guilty and punished according to the laws and usages of war, the hostages will be given up. But, if improperly retained and punished, retaliation will be resorted to

You have some Chaplains in your hands. Will you deliver them? Please send replies to the above by this flag of truce.

I am, very respectfully, your obedient servant,

WM. H LUDLOW,
Lieut. Col., and Agent for Exchange of Prisoners.

[No. 55.]

MR. OULD TO BRIG. GEN. MEREDITH.

CONFEDERATE STATES OF AMERICA, WAR DEPARTMENT, }
Richmond, Va., August 16, 1863. }

Brig. Gen. S. A. MEREDITH,
Agent of Exchange:

SIR: I respectfully call your attention to the correspondence between Lieut. Col. Ludlow and myself, in relation to Dr. Rucker and the detention of surgeons, and especially to my communication of the 23d of June last. Lieut. Col. Ludlow, in his reply, bearing date July 12, 1863, says: "As understood by me, Dr. Rucker's alleged offences were committed in west Virginia, within the territory militarily occupied at the time by the troops of the United States. If so, by the laws and usages of war, your authorities have no jurisdiction in the case."

Paragragh 59, of your general order No. 100, does not make the distinction of military occupation suggested by Lieut. Col. Ludlow. It says, "a prisoner of war remains answerable for his crimes committed against the captor's army or people, committed before he was captured, and for which he has not been punished by his own authorities." Any construction which would not include such "crimes" as are committed within the territory militarily occupied by the army to which the offender belongs, would leave the provision almost without any meaning. In Dr. Rucker's case, however, the distinction is without avail. I have delayed thus long in answering Lieut. Col. Ludlow's communication of the 12th ultimo, in order that I might obtain accurate information as to the facts in the case.

He is indicted for murder, committed on the 23d July, 1861, upon a citizen of Virginia, in Covington, Alleghany county, Va. At that time no Federal force was there, or ever had been. The United States forces did not invade that county, or region of country, until May, 1862.

He is also indicted for stealing a horse in January, 1862.

He is moreover charged with other offences, committed while the Federal forces were in the county.

Whatever, therefore, may be the construction placed upon the general order, so far as military occupation is concerned, Dr. Rucker's case is certainly embraced within the provisions of paragraph 59.

I am also reliably informed that, at the time of at least some of the offences charged against him, Dr. Rucker had no connection with your army. It will hardly be contended, I suppose, that immunity for crimes already committed, can be purchased by joining the forces of an invading army.

The correspondence between Lieut. Col. Ludlow and myself seems to indicate that the only hindrance to the immediate and unconditional release of all surgeons, is to be found in the detention of Dr. Rucker; and further, if such detention could find its justification in your general orders, even that hindrance would be removed. I therefore, bring to your attention the foregoing facts, drawn from the indictments against Dr. Rucker, by which it very clearly appears that he is rightfully held, and, therefore, Dr. Green wrongfully detained in retaliation.

I accordingly renew to you the proposition heretofore made by me, that all surgeons now held on both sides, with the exception of Dr. Rucker, be released without delay. I have no objection to extend the proposition to nurses and members of sanitary commissions. I would, however, much prefer that it should embrace all non-combatants.

I will be much obliged to you if you give me an early specific reply to the propositions herein contained.

Respectfully, your obedient servant,
RO. OULD, *Agent of Exchange.*

[No. 56.]

BRIG. GEN. MEREDITH TO MR. OULD.

HEADQUARTERS DEPARTMENT OF VIRGINIA, 7TH ARMY CORPS.
Fort Monroe, Sep. 30, 1863.

Hon. ROBERT OULD,
Agent of Exchange, Richmond, Va.:

SIR: In the hope that the officers of the medical department, on both sides, may be mutually released, who are now held as prisoners, I offer to you the following proposition: "That all persons of the medical departments, distinctly known as such, held as prisoners on either side, shall be discharged, irrespective of numbers."

If you will not agree to the above, I propose that "all shall be discharged, except one or more designated persons, for whom equivalents may be retained by the opposite party. We designate no one for exception."

Very respectfully, your obedient servant,
S. A. MEREDITH,
Brig. Gen., and Commissioner for Exchange.

[No. 57.]

MR. OULD TO BRIG. GEN. MEREDITH.

C. S. A., WAR DEPARTMENT,
Richmond, Va., Oct. 2, 1863.

Brig. Gen. S. A. MEREDITH,
Agent of Exchange:

SIR: Your proposition of the 30th ultimo, to wit, "that all persons of the medical departments, distinctly known as such, held as prisoners on either side, shall be discharged, irrespective of numbers," is substantially a proposition that the Confederate authorities shall deliver to you Dr. Wm. Rucker, who is now in the custody of the State of Virginia, for crimes committed before he had any connection with the Federal army. If it does not mean that, I will agree to it most cheerfully. If it does, I cannot.

Your alternative proposition, that "all shall be discharged, except one or more designated persons, for whom equivalents may be retained by the opposite party," is the old demand that we should consent to the retention of Dr. Green, or some other surgeon, in retaliation for Dr. Wm. Rucker. To that I cannot agree. We are either right or wrong in the retention of Rucker. If right, you ought not to hold an equivalent. If wrong, Rucker should be delivered up. In no aspect of the case should Dr. Green, or any other equivalent, be retained.

In my communication to you of August 16, last, I went very fully into the case of Dr. Rucker. Can a single statement therein contained, be successfully controverted? If not, upon what grounds can you deny our right to hold and try him? I will really be obliged to you if you will show wherein I am wrong in any of the positions assumed in my communication of the 30th of August.

When you deny our right to hold Dr. Rucker, or contend for your right to detain a hostage for him, am I to understand you as contending that no officer on either side is to be held on charges preferred against him?

If you have any surgeon in confinement, under charges, let him be retained and tried under them. I will not complain, especially if they are preferred by a grand jury, as is the case with Dr. Rucker. I, however, can never agree that any surgeon shall be held as an equivalent or hostage for Dr. Rucker.

Some doubt has been expressed as to whether Rucker was ever a surgeon, regularly in your service. How is it as to that?

Respectfully, your obedient servant,

RO. OULD, *Agent of Exchange.*

CORRESPONDENCE

Relative to the Detention of Persons captured on rivers and the high seas.

[No. 58.]

BRIG. GEN. MEREDITH TO MR. OULD.

Office Commissioner for Exchange,
Fort Monroe, Va., July 31, 1863.

Hon. Robert Ould,
 Com'r for Exchange, &c., Richmond, Va.:

Sir: On June 10th, 1863, the barque Texana, bound from New York to New Orleans, was captured and burned by one James Dake and some fifteen others, who were on board the steamer Boston, which steamer they had taken possession of the night before. The pilot of the Texana was permitted to land, but the captain and crew were taken to Mobile and from thence to Richmond, where, ever since, they have been confined in the Libby prison.

The case of these men appears to me hard in all its bearings, and I cannot believe that the authorities at Richmond would sanction such irregular procedures, or establish such an inhuman precedent, were they fully cognizant of the facts in the case. With this is a list of these prisoners, and I hope you will use your best endeavors for their immediate release.

Respectfully, your obedient servant,
 S. A. MEREDITH,
 Brig. Gen., and Commissioner for Exchange.

[No. 59.]

MR. OULD TO BRIG. GEN. MEREDITH.

Confederate States of America, War Department,
 Richmond, Va., Aug. 1, 1863.

Brig. Gen. S. A. Meredith,
 Agent of Exchange:

Sir: I have received your communication in reference to the "captain and crew of the barque Texana." In it, you speak of "irregular procedures" and "inhuman precedents." If you had been acquainted with the action of your own authorities in similar cases, you would hardly have used such language.

I refer you to the several communications of mine to Lieut. Col. Ludlow in reference to the detention of the masters and pilots of Confederate steamers, and especially to my endorsement, dated June 29th, upon his application for the release of the officers and crew of the steamer Emily. The "irregular procedures" and "inhuman precedents" are not to be found in the action of the Confederate authorities. The slightest search will disclose them elsewhere, however. You have now in your prisons the following:

Capt. Floyd and the other officers and crew of the ferry-boat De Soto. They are in prison in St. Louis, Missouri, and have been since January last.

The officers and crew of the schooner Belle, captured last February off Charleston. Some of the officers are now at Fort Lafayette.

The officers and crew of the steamer Cuba, captured off Mobile, last May. The captain is at Key West in prison.

The officers and crew of the steamer Emma Bett, captured in June last in the Sunflower river, Mississippi. They are said to be in Camp Chase. They are certainly in captivity.

The officers and crew of the steamer Brittania, captured off Charleston in July, 1863.

The officers and crew of the schooner Glide. The captain (Perry) is at Fort Lafayette.

To convince you more fully that the Confederate authorities have no desire to initiate "irregular procedures" or establish "inhuman precedents," in the direction you indicate, I propose that the officers and crews of all vessels who are now held in confinement by either the United States or the Confederate States, be immediately released, equivalents from the army to be given to the party which has the excess. This proposition practically tests who favors the "irregular procedures" and "inhuman precedents."

Respectfully, your obedient servant,
RO. OULD, *Agent of Exchange.*

[No. 60.]

BRIG. GEN. MEREDITH TO MR. OULD.

OFFICE COMMISSIONER FOR EXCHANGE,
Fort Monroe, Va., Sept. 27, 1863.

Hon. ROBERT OULD,
Agent of Exchange, Richmond, Va.:

SIR: I have written to you twice in relation to the captain and crew of the barque Texana. You say that you will release them if we will release prisoners of yours in like circumstances. We do not know of any prisoners held by us under similar circumstances as the crew of the Texana. If you will refer specifically to any such in our hands they shall be released.

   Respectfully, your obedient servant,
         S. A. MEREDITH,
    Brig. Gen., and Commissioner for Exchange.

[No 61.]

MR. OULD TO BRIG. GEN. MEREDITH.

CONFEDERATE STATES OF AMERICA, WAR DEPARTMENT,
    Richmond, Va., Sept. 28, 1863.

Brig. Gen. S. A. MEREDITH,
  Agent of Exchange:

SIR: On the 1st of August last, in reply to your first communication respecting the captain and crew of the barque Texana, I gave you a list of six captures made by the Federal forces some or all of which corresponded with that of the Texana. I refer you to the letter of August 1st. The captures were either made at sea, or in our western rivers. The parties were engaged in either exterior or interior commerce. How they differ from the officers and crew of the Texana, I cannot conceive. I then made you a proposition in reference to the release of the officers and crews of all vessels, who are now held in confinement by either the United States or Confederate States. You have not seen fit to accept it. I now make another proposal, to wit: that the officers and crews of all merchant vessels, who are now confined on either side, be immediately and unconditionally released. Either the proposal made in my letter of the 21st ult., or in this present one, will be acceptable to me.

   Respectfully, your obedient servant,
        RO. OULD, *Agent of Exchange.*

[No. 62.]

BRIG. GEN. MEREDITH TO MR. OULD.

OFFICE COMMISSIONER FOR EXCHANGE,
   Fortress Monroe, Va., Oct. 28, 1863.

Hon. ROBERT OULD,
  Agent of Exchange, Richmond, Va.:

SIR: Allow me to call your attention to the fact, that the officers and crews of the following named vessels are still detained in southern

prisons. These captures were made in January last, and the officers have been paroled and exchanged. Will you let me know by the next flag of truce, why they are not released?
U. S. ship "Morning Light."
U. S. schooner "Velocity."
U. S. steamer "Harrit Lane."

   Respectfully, your obedient servant,
       S. A. MEREDITH,
    Brig. Gen., and Commissioner for Exchange.

[No. 63.]

MR. OULD TO BRIG. GEN. MEREDITH.

       RICHMOND, Oct. 31, 1863.

Brigadier General S. A. MEREDITH,
  Agent of Exchange:

SIR: I have just received your letter of the 28th instant, making inquiry respecting "the officers and crews" of the Morning Light, Velocity and Harriet Lane. You first say they "are still detained in southern prisons." You next say "the officers have been paroled and exchanged." I really cannot see how paroled and exchanged officers can "still be detained in southern prisons." If they have been paroled and exchanged, when was it done and by whom? If I have made any agreement as to these parties, I will fulfill it to the letter.

If the officers and crews of those vessels are in confinement, they are there because you refuse to release the officers and crews of Confederate vessels. The former are very likely to remain in confinement until you release the latter, unless I have made some agreement which entitles them to a discharge. I am not aware of having done so.

   Respectfullly,
    Your obedient servant,
      RO. OULD, *Agent of Exchange.*

CORRESPONDENCE

Relative to persons held in confinement at the South under conviction by a court.

[No. 64.]

BRIG. GEN. MEREDITH TO MR. OULD.

Fort Monroe, November 15, 1863.

Hon. Robert Ould,
 Agent of Exchange, Richmond, Va.:

Sir: I have information which will be relied and acted upon as authentic, unless formally and without reserve, denied, that Joseph Sherman and Edward Ludwich, of the 4th Maine infantry, were sent to the penitentiary from Botetourt county, in October, 1862, for a term of years, and that Anderson Crawford, of a Maryland regiment, has been sent to the penitentiary also, in all three cases upon accusations not recognized as criminal according to the laws of war. A reasonable time for receiving information from the South will be allowed, before giving any special orders in these cases.

 Respectfully, your obedient servant,
   S. A. MEREDITH.

There is no such man as Crawford in the penitentiary, nor has there been such a man during my official term. The other persons named are in the penitentiary, under judgments of the circuit court of Botetourt, and there they will remain during my term of service.

   JOHN LETCHER.

November 17, 1863.

[No. 65.]

MR. OULD TO BRIG. GEN. MEREDITH.

C. S. A., War Department,
Richmond, Va., Nov. 18, 1863.

Brig. Gen. S. A. Meredith,
 Agent of Exchange:

Sir: I herewith return to you the indorsement of Governor Letcher upon your communication of the 15th instant, relating to Sherman,

Ludwick, and Crawford. I also enclose to you a copy of the record of the trial and conviction of the two first named, and a letter from the superintendent of the penitentiary. If you will inform me in what State Anderson Crawford was convicted, I will send you a similar copy of the proceedings had in his case.

So many recent and novel interpretations of the "laws of war" have been delivered, that I am at a loss to know, from the tenor of your letter, whether it is intended by your authorities to contest the right of the Commonwealth of Virginia to punish persons within her jurisdiction for felonies. If, however, your own general orders are to have any effect, I suppose paragraph 59, of general order, No 100, settles the question.

I have very frankly, and at an early day, responded to your inquiries. I hope I am not asking too much, when I request that any "special orders" which may be issued in these cases, may be promptly communicated to me.

Respectfully, your obedient servant,
ROBERT OULD,
Agent of Exchange.

CORRESPONDENCE WITH GENERAL HITCHCOCK.

[No. 66.]

MR. OULD TO BRIG. GEN. MEREDITH.

RICHMOND, VA., *Oct.* 27, 1863.

Brig. Gen. S. A. MEREDITH,
Agent of Exchange:

SIR: I enclose to you a memorandum of the paroles to which I have referred in several recent communications. Most of these paroles, you will observe, are antecedent to May 23, 1863. The reason why these paroles have not been heretofore charged, is, that up to July, 1863, we had the advantage of prisoners and paroles. Not one of these paroles is covered by any declaration of exchange, except the one lately made by you. For no one of them have I received any equivalent. All of them, since the date of your general order No. 207, were given in pursuance of a distinct agreement between the commanders of two opposing armies. I have many other paroles in my possession, but I have only presented those which are within the terms of your general orders, according to their respective dates. I understand there are other paroles coming within the same general orders, which were given by your officers and men on the other side of the Mississippi river. They, as yet, have not reached me. When they do, and when I show they are within the scope of your general orders, I will claim them. Otherwise, I will discard them.

I have also received other informal paroles, which I have sent back for correction. These are also within the provisions of your general orders. When they are returned, I will claim them also.

Respectfully, your obedient servant,
RO. OULD, *Agent of Exchange.*

[No. 67]

MAJ. GEN. HITCHCOCK TO BRIG. GEN. MEREDITH.

WASHINGTON CITY, D. C., *Nov.* 1863.

Brig. Gen. S. A. MEREDITH,
Commissioner for Exchange of Prisoners:

SIR: Your communication of the 29th ult. has been received, forwarding what "purports to be a tabular statement of the number of valid paroles," claimed by Mr. Ould, with a copy of his letter accompanying it to yourself, of the 24th ult.

This tabular statement covers a claim to 18,867 paroles of Federal troops, without distinctions of grade, no officers or non-commissioned officers being noticed as among the prisoners. The statement professes to enumerate forty-four places where captures were made, with the names of captors, and dates of captures—the number said to have been captured being carried out in figures.

This statement may include some prisoners captured and paroled according to the laws of war, but if so, it is impossible to distinguish them by any evidence in the statement itself. A few are said to have been "receipted for" at Baton Rouge, January 22, 1863, and February 14, 1863, which may be verified, and some evidences may come to light confirming the alleged captures by Generals Lee, Bragg, and, possibly, some others; but, on the whole, the statement is unsatisfactory, and in its present form, is regarded as without credit, and not entitled to consideration.

The statement does not show, in any one instance, by whom the prisoners were received, or to whom, or even where, they were delivered, leaving it to be presumed that they were, for the most part, paroled on the instant of capture, without authority under the cartel, in not being "reduced to actual possession," contrary to both the laws of war, as set forth in order No. 100, of 1863, and the provisions of the cartel. Order No. 100 merely publishes the laws of war, and the cartel is entirely in harmony with it.

The orders on this subject subsequently issued, and to which Mr. Ould appeals, were expressly designed to give effect to those laws and to the cartel, and were in no manner intended to abrogate, and neither do they abrogate or modify the one or the other.

If the enemy wishes, in good faith, to carry out the orders he refers to, the proper course would be to issue similar orders, and for a like purpose, in which case there might be some hope of a compliance with both the cartel and the laws of war.

Mr. Ould's effort to have recognized certain paroles as valid, which have been informally and improperly made, embracing, so far as we can know from his statements, many *citizens* in Kentucky, Tennessee, and elsewhere, (no particular placed being named in some instances,) by appealing to northern orders, is a mere perversion of the clear and manifest design of those orders, that design being, as already stated, to enforce, and not to nullify the laws of war. We appeal to those orders, and intend to be guided by them, and if the enemy would assume them, and be governed by them also, all difficulties on the subject of paroles would cease. By Mr. Ould's mode of application or misapplication of those orders, he would use them to destroy, and not enforce the laws of war.

The laws of war are first in order, imposing obligations upon belligerents, and they continue to be obligatory upon both parties, unless modified by a special agreement under a cartel, which, when agreed upon, becomes the highest authority in all specified cases included in the cartel, leaving the laws of war in full operation in all cases not provided for in such cartel—a cartel being analagous to a treaty of commerce between nations, which may modify the natural laws of trade or commerce, binding both parties to the treaty.

The orders of a general in the field, or of a general in chief of one of the belligerents, is only operative within the field of the general's command, and can have no effect to modify either the laws of war or the provisions of a particular cartel. Such orders are purely disciplinary in the army where issued, and can neither bind an enemy, nor can an enemy appeal to them to justify his departure from, or violation of, either a particular cartel or the laws of war. A departure from such an order within the army subject to the authority issuing the order, might subject the offender to punishment within his own army, but could not be appealed to to make a parole valid, which by the laws of war, or by the provisions of a particular cartel, would be disowned as not valid.

While we set forth these principles as binding, we deny, emphatically, that the orders appealed to by Mr. Ould sanction his departure from the laws of war or the cartel—the express purpose of order No. 207 (1-63) being to enforce the provisions of the existing cartel. It sets out by an appeal, in paragraph I, to the cartel, by its date and the date of the order by which it was published, the provisions of which are to be enforced, and this is again set forward in paragraph II. Order No. 207 publishes a very important law of war in paragraph II, in announcing that "the obligations imposed by the general laws and usages of war upon the non-combatant inhabitants of a section of country passed over by an invading army, cease when the military occupation ceases; and any pledge or parole given by such persons, in regard to future service, is null and of no effect." This paragraph of order No. 207, does not originate, it merely announces the law of war on the subject to which it refers, but it is particularly significant in view of the probable character of many of the paroles claimed as valid in the tabular statement furnished by Mr. Ould, in which, under the head of "where captured," the statement uses generalities which can in no sense be received. Thus, captures are said to have been made in "Kentucky and Tennessee;" in "Tennessee;" in "Kentucky and Tennessee" (again;) in "Tennessee," (again;) in "Kentucky and Tennessee," (a third time;) in "Barbour county, Kentucky," (wether soldiers or citizens we cannot tell,) in "Western Virginia;" in "Western Virginia," (again;) in "Hinds county, Mississippi;" in "Eastern Virginia;" in "Mississippi;" in "Kentucky and Tennessee," (for the fourth time,) &c.

In fine the statement is wholly informal and without authority.

You will please furnish Mr. Ould a certified copy of this communication. Very respectfully, your obedient servant,

E. A. HITCHCOCK,
Maj. Gen. Vols. and Commissioner for the Exchange of Prisoners.

FORT MONROE, VA., Nov. 9, 1863.

A true copy. S. A. MEREDITH,
Brig. Gen. and Commissioner for Exchange.

[No. 68.]

MR. OULD TO BRIG. GEN. MEREDITH.

C. S. A., War Department,
Richmond, Va., Nov. 21, 1863.

Brig. Gen. S. A. Meredith,

Agent of Exchange:

Sir: I have received the letter of General Hitchcock relating to the memorandum of paroles which I forwarded to you.

General Hitchcock seems to have misapprehended my purpose somewhat in sending you that memorandum. You requested a list of the paroles which I claimed, and the paper which I sent to you was only intended to be understood as a memorandum in the way of notice to you. I did not expect you to agree to recognize the paroles therein referred to in such a general way, upon the mere presentation of the paper. The evidence which supports that memorandum of paroles is on file in my office. If we could only have agreed upon the principle by which they should be computed and adjusted, all the rest would have been easy work. I would have presented the paroles themselves or authenticated lists of them. The fact that they were given, the circumstances under which they were given, the parties giving them, would all appear upon the face of the papers in proper form. As General Hitchcock seems to indicate a willingness to re-open this matter, I will state for his benefit frankly, the principles by which I propose to be governed.

1. I will not claim the paroles of citizens. All the paroles which I will produce will be those of Federal soldiers in actual service at the time of capture.

2. I will show the particular locality where the parties were captured, the command to which they belong, the command which captured them, and the precise date of each transaction.

3. I will accompany the presentation with such full and particular evidence as will enable you to verify the truth of the case by your own records and the statements of your own officers and soldiers.

4. More than thirty of the forty-four items in my memorandum are cases of captures made previous to the 22d May, 1863. It has never, at any time, been alleged that I had any notice before that time that paroling upon the battle field was not to be permitted. The Federal authorities have charged against me paroles taken upon the battle field up to that date, and have received credit for them. I would have received credit for these items many months ago if you had have had paroles or prisoners of ours to have offsetted against them. I will thank General Hitchcock to inform me, upon what principle he can reject those thirty-odd items. If he wants evidence that I have allowed precisely similar paroles, I will furnish it.

5. As to such of the paroles as were given between the 22d May, 1863, and the 3d of July, (the date of general order, No. 207,) I shall

contend that they shall be allowed under the provisions of paragraph 131, of general order, No. 100. I will allow any similar paroles given to you during the same period.

6. As to all paroles given after the 3d of July, 1863, I will allow general order, No. 207, to have full force. No paroles from and after that date are to be valid, unless the paroling is in pursuance of the agreement of the commanders of two opposing armies.

7. In my memorandum the officers and non-commissioned officers are reduced to *privates*. There are but very few, if any, commissioned officers on the lists. They have already been exchanged and checked off. This is of itself proof that your authorities have heretofore recognized these paroles. The lists and paroles will show the grade of all the parties.

8. I have been greatly misunderstood by General Hitchcock, if he thinks I have refused to be governed by your general orders. Gen. Hitchcock says: "we appeal to those orders, and intend to be governed by them, and if the enemy would assume them, and be governed by them also, all difficulties on the subject of paroles would cease." I have already expressed my willingness to be governed by your "general orders" on the subject of paroles." It was my original proposition—I adhere to it still. Let, then, "all difficulties cease."

9. If our present difficulties are to cease, let me for the sake of future harmony suggest that there be some definitive meaning attached to the phrase "commanders of two opposing armies." Who are such commanders? We can readily understand that General Lee and General Meade are such. But is General Thomas the commander of one of the opposing armies at Chattanooga, or is it General Grant? Was General Pemberton the commander of an opposing army, when he was subject to the orders of General Johnston who was in his immediate neighborhood? Was General Gardiner the commander of an opposing army at Port Hadson? If so, is not every one who holds a separate command, such a commander? Does size constitute an army? If a Captain or Lieutenant is on detached service, is he the commander of an opposing army, and can he be released on parole by an agreement made with the officer who captured him, if he also is on detached service? I make these inquiries of General Hitchcock in no captious spirit. They do present difficulties to my mind, and I should like to know what is to be considered as the true interpretation of the phrase. All the captures after the 3d of July, 1863, which I ask you to recognize, were in pursuance of "an agreement between the commanders of two opposing armies." I cannot see how any difficulty can arise between General Hitchcock and myself after his letter, except as to captures between May 22d, 1863, and July 3d, 1863. They are but very few in number.

I will thank you to send this letter or a copy of it to General Hitchcock.

    Respectfully, your obedient servant,

                              RO. OULD.

                              Agent of Exchange.

[No. 69.]

MAJ. GEN HITCHCOCK TO BRIG. GEN. MEREDITH.

WASHINGTON CITY, Dec. 28th, 1863.

Brig Gen S. A. MEREDITH,
Com'r for Exchange of Prisoners:

SIR: I have read the copy you forwarded of Mr. Ould's communication of the 21st inst., in which, I perceive, Mr. Ould thinks I misapprehended his purpose in forwarding the "tabular statement" of alleged valid paroles, made chiefly in the West and South. I supposed that the *tabular statement* was sent to you in explanation of the large number of prisoners declared exchanged by Mr. Ould, the propriety of which had been very properly questioned by you. If that was not the purpose of the statement, I regret that it fell under my notice. If Mr. Ould wishes either to present another "statement," or to furnish detailed explanations of that already before us, it will be time enough to consider the points he may raise when he presents them. In the meantime, I think it necessary to observe that neither Mr. Ould, yourself, nor myself, have powers outside of the cartel, except those plainly necessary for the execution of its provisions; but, in this connection, I must affirm that the first *shock* given to the free and unbiased execution of the provisions of the cartel, came from Mr. Davis, in his "message" of the 12th of January, of the present year, in which he declares his purpose of delivery to the several State authorities South, all commissioned officers of the Federal army who may be captured, to be tried, under State laws, for the crime of exciting servile insurrection. This stands yet as the avowed purpose of the chief executive of the States engaged in the rebellion. It has not been annulled in any form whatever, nor has the act of the southern Congress, in support of Mr. Davis' views, been in any manner repealed or disavowed. Without looking any further, I appeal to this as a full justification of the Federal commander in-chief in suspending the operation of that portion of article four, of the cartel, which requires "all prisoners of war to be discharged on parole in ten days after their capture," it being manifest, that the authorities South could not parole prisoners according to the cartel, and carry out their declared purpose of delivering the officers over to State authorities to be tried as *criminals* under State laws. Whatever may have been the reason why the declared purpose of Mr. Davis has not been extensively carried into effect, the fact of the existence of that purpose, sanctioned as we know it to have been, is a sufficient reason on our part for not delivering prisoners on parole, particularly as there is every reason to believe that the purpose of Mr. Davis has only been arrested by the fact, that, by the fortune of war, we had in our hands more prisoners than were held in the South. In addition to the above, the treatment of colored troops, which make an integral portion of the Federal army, when captured in the South, is too well known to permit us for a moment to suppose, in the present state of things, that there is any design in the South to treat that class of troops according to the laws of war, applicable to other troops of the Federal army; and until the southern authorities make some distinct declaration of a purpose to treat colored troops and their officers, in the employment of the United States Government, in all respects, according to the laws of war, as applicable to other troops, we cannot recede from the position taken by the commander-in-chief above referred to. The wisdom and the necessity of existing orders on this subject, will sufficiently defend the measure in view of the *threats* and *practices* of the South, which only need to be known to justify this measure.

It is very well known that Colonel Ludlow made these subjects the frequent topic of conversation with Mr. Ould, without producing any impression on Mr. Ould, tending to the point of inducing a declaration, by authority, from the South, that all officers of the Federal army, as well as enlisted men, shall receive, when captured, the treatment due to prisoners of war, with the express declaration that colored officers and men, shall receive similar treatment.

You will please communicate these views to Mr. Ould, with a request that he will lay them before his Government.

Respectfully, your obedient servant,
E. A. HITCHCOCK,
Major Gen. Vols. and Commissioner for Exchange.

A true copy.

S. A. MEREDITH,
Brigadier General and Commissioner of Exchange.

[No. 70.]

MAJ. GEN. HITCHCOCK TO BRIG. GEN. MEREDITH.

WASHINGTON CITY, D. C.,
November 13, 1863.

Brig. Gen. S. MEREDITH,
Commissioner for Exchange of Prisoners:

SIR: I am not yet informed whether any, or how far, relief may have reached our unfortunate prisoners of war in Richmond and its vicinity, under the orders of the Secretary of War, to send supplies to them of both food and clothing.

Meantime, it is proper and necessary that Mr. Ould should be notified, for the information of his Government, that whatever steps may have been, or may be taken thus to extend relief, must, on no consideration, be appealed to by the enemy to relieve him from the obligation to treat prisoners of war according to the laws of civilized warfare.

If, in other words, our prisoners in Richmond fail to receive such supplies as the laws alike of humanity and war require, the authorities in Richmond must be informed, that it will not be considered a valid explanation or excuse for them to appeal to the fact, should it exist, that supplies from us have not reached them.

The action of our Government in this matter is dictated purely by humanity, and is only an effort to relieve our prisoners from suffering inflicted upon them contrary to the claims of both humanity and the laws of war, and must not be understood as relieving the authorities at Richmond from responsibility to the Christian world in the premises.

If the authorities in Richmond will send us these prisoners we will not only feed and clothe them, but will continue to supply food and clothing as heretofore to such prisoners as may be in our possession; and you will propose to Mr. Ould, that, in this case, we will agree without any reserve, to respect the parole they may give according to the laws of war, from which they shall not be relieved in view of past differences or pending questions on the subject of exchange, without the previously obtained consent of the authorities represented by Mr. Ould, as a cut for exchanges, under the cartel.

You will please lose no time in communicating a copy of this note, certified by yourself to Mr. Ould, and will urge upon him its acceptance, as due to the most solemn considerations in the face of the civilized world.

Very respectfully,
Your obedient servant,
E. A. HITCHCOCK,
Maj. Gen. Vols., and Commissioner for Exchange of Prisoners.
FORT MONROE, VA., *Nov.* 15, 1863.

A true copy.
S. A. MEREDITH, *Brig. Gen. and Commissioner for Exchange.*

[No. 71.]

MR. OULD TO BRIG. GEN. MEREDITH.

CONFEDERATE STATES OF AMERICA, WAR DEPARTMENT,
Richmond, Va., Nov. 18, 1863.

Brig. Gen. S. A. MEREDITH,
Agent of Exchange:

SIR: The letter of General Hitchcock has been received.

Until the Confederate authorities appear to be released "from the obligation to treat prisoners of war according to the laws of civilized warfare," or offer as "an explanation or excuse" for insufficient food that supplies have not been forwarded by your Government, it is entirely unnecessary to discuss what will be the views of your authorities in either contingency.

Statements, most infamously false, have recently been made and circulated at the North, by persons whose calling should have imposed a respect for truth, which their own personal honor seems to have failed to secure. Our regulations require that prisoners shall receive the same rations as soldiers in the field. Such your prisoners have received and will continue to receive. Do you ask more? If so, what do you demand? We recognize, in the fullest form, our obligation to treat your prisoners with humanity, and to serve them with the same food, in quantity and quality, as is given to our own soldiers. If the supply is scanty, you have only to blame the system of warfare you have waged against us. There is nothing in the action of the Confederate Government which gives any sort of countenance to the charge of cruelty or inhumanity to your prisoners. In the first place, we have importuned you to agree to a fair and honest proposition which would secure the release of all of them. When that was rejected, you have been permitted to send, without stint or limitation, all kinds of supplies to them.

General Hitchcock requests that the prisoners now in our hands be returned to your lines. This is not accompanied with any proposition to release our prisoners now in your hands. So far from that being the case, he promises to "continue to supply food and clothing as heretofore" to such. General Hitchcock need not have urged you to "lose no time in communicating" his letter. No degree of haste would have secured the assent of the Confederate authorities to a proposition so flagrantly unequal. We are ready to relieve your Government from the burthen of supplying "food and clothing as heretofore," to our people in your hands, and if they are sent to us, yours shall be returned to you—the excess on one side or the other to be on parole. I hope you will "urge" upon General Hitchcock the acceptance of this proposition "as due to the most solemn considerations in the face of the civilized world." We are content that the "civilized world" should draw its own conclusions when it contrasts the two offers. I will thank you to forward this communication to General Hitchcock, or inform him that the Confederate authorities decline to accept his proposition.

Respectfully, your obedient servant,

RO. OULD,
Agent of Exchange.

[No. 72.]

GEN. HITCHCOCK TO GEN. MEREDITH.

WASHINGTON CITY, D. C., Nov. 23d, 1863.

Brig. Gen. S. A. MEREDITH,
Commissioner for Exchange of Prisoners:

SIR: Your note forwarding a copy of Mr. Ould's letter of the 18th instant, addressed to yourself, as an answer to my letter of the 13th, has been received. Mr. Ould, I perceive, states that our prisoners in Richmond receive "the same rations as soldiers in the field," according to the regulations."

The "regulations" may be such as Mr. Ould states them to be, but that our prisoners receive "rations" as stated, is contradicted by all of the evidence that has reached me outside of Mr. Ould's statement; and the evidence rests upon the statements of eye witnesses and of actual sufferers under the treatment received in Richmond and at Belle Isle, besides the testimony of facts disclosed by the visible condition of a delivery of some one hundred and eighty prisoners made at City Point, many of whom died, before reaching Fort Monroe, from *starvation*, according to the judgment of a competent medical officer.

Upon the evidence above stated, the Secretary of War ordered supplies to be sent for the distribution to the remaining prisoners; and this state of things induced the letter of the 13th instant, proposing to receive on parole the prisoners, and to hold them off duty till exchanged, independently of all existing difficulties on the subject of exchange.

Mr. Ould declines this offer and proposes that, if we will send to the South the prisoners in our hands, they will send ours and the excess on one side or the other to be on parole."

Whatever appearance of verbal fairness there may be in this, the conduct of Mr. Ould, in connection with recent declarations of exchange, will not permit us to regard this proposal as made in good faith and we cannot rely upon its being carried out by the enemy.

In the first place, the proclamation of Mr. Davis, and other public acts of those in power in the South, remain in full force, so far as we know, and are actually being enforced in the South, by which distinction is made between classes of troops employed by the United States and officers, serving with colored troops, if taken prisoners, do not receive and are not to receive the treatment due to prisoners of war, whilst the enlisted men of colored troops, when taken prisoners, it has been publicly declared, shall be sold into slavery.

That this distinction is made *actual*, in the treatment of prisoners of war, we know in some cases, and have much reason to apprehend it in others, which have not been permitted to see the light. We have positive information of the fact, that two colored seamen of the United States marine were captured near Charleston, and were not treated as prisoners of war.

Two free colored young men, with a Massachusetts regiment, were captured near Galveston and publicly sold into slavery.

In a recent case I made a proposal to release, mutually, all chaplains; and the proposal was "cheerfully accepted;" but, lthough we delivered about or more than twice the number we received, the enemy held back the chaplain of a Massachusetts colored regiment who was confined and in irons at Columbia, S. C.

In addition to these facts, Mr. Ould, not long since, declared that he would proceed to make declarations of exchange whenever he conscientiously felt that he had the right to do so, for the purpose of putting men into the field.

If this announcement means anything at all, it means that the usages of war, and the express provisions of the cartel, are subordinate to the individual determination and purposes of Mr. Ould on the subject of declarations of exchange; and, as a consequence, we must suppose that if Mr. Ould can obtain possession of the "excess" of prisoners, now in our possession, he will "proceed" to declare them exchanged, and put them into the field, upon what he might allege as his sense of right. When called upon for an explanation he would prepare what he might call a "tabular statement of paroles," as he recently did, made up from guerilla captures of citizens in remote parts of the country, set down as captured at *such places* as *Kentucky*, as *Tennessee*, as *Mississippi*, or at such a place as *Kentucky* and *Tennessee*, not in any instance properly reporting to whom delivered. Mr. Ould has shown the latitudinarian construction he puts upon his powers, and the nature of his sense of *right*, by writing a letter on the 10th of Oct. which he has not thought it necessary to communicate to us, but which has been published in a Richmond paper, by which he took upon himself the power to declare that the whole number of men delivered by General Banks, at Mobile, embracing several thousand men, captured at Port Hudson, were under no obligation to preserve their parole.

Mr. Ould has been a mere agent under the cartel, and when a question comes up as to the import of the cartel, its meaning, &c., Mr. Ould has no power to decide the question, for that belongs to the parties by whose authority the cartel was made.

The cartel provided two places for the delivery of prisoners of war, City Point and Vicksburg; but it provided, also, that when these places, or either of them, should become unavailable by the exigencies of war, some other point might be agreed upon.

Vicksburg, having fallen into our hands, became unavailable, as contemplated by the cartel, and Gen. Banks agreed with the rebel commander in the field that Gen. Banks would deliver the Port Hudson prisoners on parole, and they were delivered accordingly.

Mr. Ould knew that those men were unconditionally in the hands of Gen. Banks. They had been "reduced to possesion," and had been taken to New Orleans, and might have been sent north, if Gen. Banks, had pleased. Instead of sending them to the North to swell the number of prisoners of war, in our hands at the North, Gen. Banks confided in the honor of a rebel commander, and "agreed" to parole those men at Mobile, Vicksburg being by the exigencies of war, no longer available as a place of delivery.

In that state of things Mr. Ould takes upon himself to decide that the delivery at Mobile was invalid, that place not being named in the cartel for the delivery of prisoners.

With a sense of right so obtuse, as this act indicates, it is doing no injustice to Mr. Ould to say that we cannot confide in any pledge he would make to carry out a special agreement, and we must accordingly decline to acquiesce in any measure which would throw into his hands a large body of prisoners of war under parole, to be by him released from its obligations according to his sense of right.

You will understand from the above statements that Mr. Ould's decision touching the prisoners delivered by Gen. Banks, is not recognized as justifiable or valid, and that we claim that they are still prisoners of war on parole.

Very respectfully,
Your obedient servant,
E. A. HITCHCOCK,
Maj. Gen. of Vol., and Com'r for Exchange of Prisoners.

THE CARTEL.

[No. 73.]

HAXALL'S LANDING, ON JAMES RIVER,
July 22, 1863.

The undersigned having been commissioned by the authorities they respectively represent, to make arrangements for a general exchange of prisoners of war, have agreed to the following articles:

ARTICLE 1. It is hereby agreed and stipulated, that all prisoners of war held by either party, including those taken on private armed vessels, known as privateers, shall be exchanged upon the conditions and terms following:

Prisoners to be exchanged man for man and officer for officer; privateers to be placed upon the footing of officers and men of the navy.

Men and officers of lower grades, may be exchanged for officers of a higher grade and men and officers of different services, may be exchanged according to the following scale of equivalents.

A general commanding in chief, or an admiral, shall be exchanged for officers of equal rank or for sixty privates or common seamen.

A flag officer or major general shall be exchanged for officers of equal rank or for forty privates or common seamen.

A commodore, carrying a broad pennant, or a brigadier general shall be exchanged for officers of equal rank or twenty privates or common seamen.

A captain in the navy or a colonel, shall be exchanged for officers of equal rank or for fifteen privates or common seamen.

A lieutenant colonel or a commander in the navy, shall be exchanged for officers of equal rank or for ten privates or common seamen.

A lieutenant commander or a major, shall be exchange for officers of equal rank or eight privates or common seamen.

A lieutenant or a master in the navy or a captain in the army or marines, shall be exchanged for officers of equal rank or six privates or common seamen.

Master's mates in the navy, or lieutenants and ensigns in the army, shall be exchanged for officers of equal rank or four privates or common seamen.

Midshipmen, warrant officers in the navy, masters of merchant vessels and commanders of privateers, shall be exchanged for officers of equal rank or three privates or common seamen; second captains, lieutenants or mates of merchant vessels or privateers and all petty officers in the navy and all non-commissioned officers in the army or marines, shall be severally exchanged for persons of equal rank or for two privates or common seamen; and private soldiers or common sea men, shall be exchanged for each other, man for man.

ARTICLE 2. Local, state, civil and militia rank held by persons not in actual military service, will not be recognized; the basis of exchange being the grade actually held in the naval and military service of the respective parties.

ARTICLE 3. If citizens held by either party on charges of disloyalty or any alleged civil offence are exchanged, it shall only be for citizens. Captured sutlers, teamsters, and all civilians in the actual service of either party to be exchanged for persons in similar position.

ARTICLE 4. All prisoners of war to be discharged on parole in ten days after their capture, and the prisoners now held and those hereafter taken to be transported to the points mutually agreed upon, at the expense of the capturing party. The surplus prisoners, not exchanged, shall not be permitted to take up arms again, nor to serve as military police, or constabulary force in any fort, garrison, or fields work, held by either of the respective parties, nor as guards of prisons, depots, or stores, nor to discharge any duty usually performed by soldiers, until exchanged under the provisions of this cartel. The exchange is not to be considered complete until the officer or soldier exchanged for has been actually restored to the lines to which he belongs.

ARTICLE 5. Each party, upon the discharge of prisoners of the other party, is authorized to discharge an equal number of their own officers or men from parole, furnishing at the same time to the other party a list of their prisoners discharged, and of their own officers and men relieved from parole; thus enabling each party to relieve from parole such of their own officers and men as the party may choose. The lists thus mutually furnished will keep both parties advised of the true condition of the exchange of prisoners.

ARTICLE 6. The stipulations and provisions above mentioned to be of binding obligation during the continuance of the war, it matters not which party may have the surplus of prisoners, the great principles involved being: 1st. An equitable exchange of prisoners, man for man, officer for officer, or officers of higher grade, exchanged for officers of lower grade, or for privates, according to the scale of equivalents. 2d. That privates and officers and men of different services may be exchanged according to the same scale of equivalents. 3d. That all prisoners, of whatever arm of service, are to be exchanged or paroled in ten days from the time of their capture, if it be practicable to transfer them to their own lines in that time; if not, as soon thereafter as practicable. 4th. That no officer, soldier, or employee in service of either party is to be considered as exchanged and absolved from his parole until his equivalent has actually reached the lines of his friends. 5th. That the parole forbids the performance of field, garrison, police, or guard, or constabulary duty.

JOHN A. DIX,
Major General.
D. H. HILL,
Major General, C. S. A.

SUPPLEMENTARY ARTICLES.

ARTICLE 7. All prisoners of war now held on either side, and all prisoners hereafter taken, shall be sent, with all reasonable dispatch, to A. M. Aiken's, below Dutch Gap, on the James river, in Virginia, or to Vicksburg, on the Mississippi river, in the State of Mississippi, and there exchanged, or paroled until such exchange can be effected, notice being previously given by each party of the number of prisoners it will send, and the time when they will be delivered at those points respectively; and in case the vicissitudes of war shall change the military relations of the places designated in this article to the contending parties, so as to render the same inconvenient for the delivery and exchange of prisoners, other places, bearing as nearly as may be the present local relations of said places to the lines of said parties, shall be, by mutual agreement, substituted. But nothing in this article contained shall prevent the commanders of two opposing armies from exchanging prisoners, or releasing them on parole, at other points mutually agreed on by said commanders.

ARTICLE 8. For the purpose of carrying into effect the foregoing articles of agreement, each party will appoint two agents, to be called agents for the exchange of prisoners of war, whose duty it shall be to communicate with each other, by correspondence and otherwise; to prepare the lists of prisoners; to attend to the delivery of the prisoners at the places agreed on, and to carry out promptly, effectually, and in good faith, all the details and provisions of the said articles of agreement.

ARTICLE 9. And in case any misunderstanding shall arise in regard to any clause or stipulation in the foregoing articles, it is mutually agreed that such misunderstanding shall not interrupt the release of prisoners on parole, as herein provided, but shall be made the subject of friendly explanation, in order that the object of this agreement may neither be defeated or postponed.

JOHN A DIX,
Major General.
D. H. HILL,
Major General C. S. A.

www.ingramcontent.com/pod-product-compliance
Lightning Source LLC
Chambersburg PA
CBHW020300090426
42735CB00009B/1153